PRAISE FOR THE **MAR**

This book is full of practical direction. I am asked, "How can I use what I do for God's glory? If you have ever asked that question, you need to read this book. It provides the "HOW TO's" with practical examples in an easy-to-read style. It's all here.

—**KEN ELDRED,** Entrepreneur and Author of
The Integrated Life, God is at Work, and *On Kingdom Business*

In *The Marketplace Christian,* Darren Shearer has given us a practical book to apply our faith to our work life by understanding and applying our spiritual gifts to our work life call. Darren has given us much more by helping us apply God's principles of manifesting Christ in our work life call. I encourage you to read and apply what Darren shares in this book.

—**OS HILLMAN,** Author of *Change Agent* and the
TGIF Today God Is First devotional

Shearer convinces us that our spiritual gifts work best at work! He challenges us to be so good and so excellent at our seemingly unspiritual talents and abilities that our faith and beliefs as Christians cannot be ignored or pushed aside. Then, he finishes it off by unpacking each spiritual gift pointedly and briefly yet thoroughly. As a pastor, I feel so served by Darren Shearer and this book. This will surely become one of my best resources as I lead marketplace Christians into their destinies.

—**BEN WARD,** Pastor of River Life Church

The Marketplace Christian by Darren Shearer is an absolute MUST read for every Christian in business, whether you're employed or an entrepreneur. Darren did an extraordinary job revealing the identity and purpose of Christians in the marketplace, plus providing both insight and tools for how to be a transformation agent in your industry to the glory of God through your spiritual gifts. Read it once, then read it again, and be a blessing by gifting a copy to someone else.

—**SHAE BYNES,** Founder of *Kingdom Driven Entrepreneur*

The Marketplace Christian powerfully fills a huge gap in the business as missions movement: how every believer can quickly identify and release their unique and anointed spiritual gifts at work! Incredibly timely and much needed. Darren beautifully weaves together how to understand, identify, and release your spiritual gifts at work. A must read for any believer who longs for a simple, powerful way to uncover and integrate their spiritual DNA at work. Darren teaches us how natural it can be to live out our spiritual gifts at work. How I wish all believers in business would read this book, embrace its teachings, and release its truths.

—**DR. JIM HARRIS,** Author of *Our Unfair Advantage: Unleash the Power of the Holy Spirit in Your Business*

Practical, practical, practical! This will be your practical guide to applying your spiritual gifts in your occupation. Darren debunks any myths that are out there about marketplace Christianity. This is a fantastic resource to help you to be successful in all your endeavors God's way.

—**TYLER MCCART,** Business owner and Host of *The Success Edge Podcast*

One of the biggest misconceptions in the faith of Christ followers today is that their day to day occupation doesn't matter; it's only what they do on Sundays at church that matters. In his latest Book, *The Marketplace Christian: A Practical Guide to Using Your Spiritual Gifts in Business*, Darren Shearer draws an amazing picture of the business calling and how we have been equipped with specific spiritual gifts to not only bless our businesses but our industries with the gifts given to us by our Heavenly Father. This is a book that will go on top of the list for our *Business...His Way* group and will be highlighted on *iWork4Him* radio. Every Christ follower out there in the marketplace needs to read this book. What a huge source of encouragement and challenge.

—JIM BRANGENBERG, Founder & Host of *iWork4Him* radio

There are lots of debates and confusion in the Body of Christ about the role of the Christian in business. However, in this book, Darren does a masterful job of showing that marketplace ministry looks different depending on the spiritual gifts God has given you for the marketplace. If you want to discover your assignment in the marketplace, then I highly recommend this book.

—AMOS JOHNSON JR., PHD
Founder, *Church for Entrepreneurs Podcast*
Author, *Take Control of Your Financial Destiny*

THE
MARKETPLACE
CHRISTIAN

A Practical Guide to
Using Your Spiritual Gifts in Business

DARREN SHEARER

HIGH BRIDGE BOOKS
HOUSTON

For my beloved wife, Marie,
and two beloved sons, Solomon and Armand

Contents

FROM SEMINARY TO RUNNING A BUSINESS

WHEN I ONCE SHARED WITH A BUSINESSMAN at a networking event that I was in seminary, studying theology in preparation for going into business, he responded without hesitation, "Does that mean you're planning to become a televangelist?" Many of my fellow Christians have been equally as baffled as to how theological training is relevant to the marketplace. What does the Christian life have to do with business?

I explained to this businessman that, in preparation for entering the world of business, I was studying "*Practical* Theology."

With a look of genuine surprise on his face, he responded candidly, "I didn't know theology was 'practical.'"

Our *theology* is our understanding of God. If our theology isn't *practical*—if it doesn't make a difference in our everyday lives beyond a religious institution—what good is it?

As the son of a pastor and a music minister, I grew up in church in Columbia, South Carolina, thinking that "ministry" was something that happened inside the walls of a church building.

Following the attacks on the World Trade Center on 9/11/01, I joined the U.S. Air Force as an officer to serve my country. However, I didn't view military service as a context in which to serve God... at least, not at first. To be sure that I was doing "ministry work" while I served in the Air Force, I served in as many church ministry roles as time permitted. I became a part-time youth pastor in a local church. I led teams of young adults on evangelistic street outreaches in downtown Shreveport, Louisiana. I led the worship music for a church service at a Spanish-speaking church. I served as a parking lot attendant at my church on Sunday mornings. I was doing all of these things during the same season of my life, trying to reassure myself that I was "doing the Lord's work."

As I was leaving Barksdale Air Force Base in Bossier City, Louisiana after work one day, heading to serve at my local church, God spoke to my heart. He said, "Right now, your full-time ministry is on this Air Force base." In that moment, exiting through the gate of my workplace, God took the limits off of my definition of "ministry."

From that point on, I began to witness God revealing himself to my co-workers, my fellow military members, in our workplace. They were asking questions about the Christian faith. They were becoming disciples of Jesus. I started using my spiritual gifts in my workplace without even realizing they were spiritual gifts. Prior to that time, I thought spiritual gifts were only for use in an institutional church setting.

When I arrived on my assignment to Kuwait during Operation Iraqi Freedom, I used my spiritual gift of *administration* to restore order and excellence in a unit that, under the command of the previous officer-in-charge, had become both a disaster and an embarrassment. The previous officer-in-charge faced disciplinary action as a result. Within two months of assuming command, my unit was named "Team of the Month" for the entire Group, which consisted of approximately 3,000 personnel. This successful turnaround of my unit opened doors of influence for me to influence my superiors, subordinates, and peers for the glory of God for the duration of that assignment.

During that same assignment, I used my spiritual gift of *teaching* to start a personal growth workshop with public support and participation from the Wing Commander of the entire base. At these "Life Enrichment Seminars," I and several other officers and enlisted personnel presented short speeches on subjects such as personal finance, physical fitness, leadership, and relationships. This gave the people opportunities to practice public speaking as well as to share valuable personal growth teaching with our fellow military members.

I was beginning to realize that the workplace is where disciples are made. I was learning that the workplace is the primary place where a Christian's spiritual gifts ought to be used. Why? Because the workplace is where we spend most of our waking hours. It is where the Christian life is modeled and observed by the world.

The Most Important Thing I Learned in Seminary

Following the Air Force, God opened a door for me to attend seminary for theological training at Regent University in Virginia Beach, Virginia. Unlike most of my classmates, I didn't enter seminary with the goal of becoming a seminary professor, pastor, or the leader of a faith-based nonprofit. I viewed seminary as a launch pad for ministry in the marketplace. I approached seminary with the understanding that my ministry would be primarily in the world of business… not inside a religious institution.

Although 85 percent of most pastors' congregations work in for-profit companies, there were not any classes about the "Theology of Business" in my seminary at the time I attended. (Fortunately, in Fall of 2015, Regent University's Divinity School added a concentration in "Marketplace Ministry" to help Christian leaders to partner with God in business.) At the time, there were not any classes about how to help Christians use their spiritual gifts in their workplaces.

However, I believe that my primary purpose for attending seminary was to make one important discovery. Through a course titled "Biblical Models of Discipleship," God revealed to me that my primary responsibility as a Christian is to make disciples of Jesus. This is the Great Commission: "make disciples of all nations" (Matt. 28:19). It's not primarily about getting people to attend church services. It's not primarily about making money for noble purposes. Yes, those things are parts of it. At the core, though, it's about making disciples, showing people what Jesus looks like. It's about knowing Him and making Him known throughout every aspect of our lives and throughout every aspect of culture.

Starting Businesses to Make Disciples

Not only did God call me to work in the marketplace, he called me to start businesses. As I learned in seminary, the entire purpose for these businesses would be to make disciples of Jesus. (In the chapters ahead, I will explain what I mean by "making disciples through a business" as well as how to do it.)

Following seminary, I went to business school at Pace University (New York City) where I became immersed in today's entrepreneurship culture. While in the Masters of Business Administration (M.B.A.) program, I was led to believe that the only respectable businesses one could start were tech companies that required millions of dollars in venture capital funding (i.e. Facebook, Google, etc.). For this reason, most of my efforts to start my first company were focused on pleasing investors rather than on pleasing God by doing what He had called and gifted me to do. I had been trying to start a business that was focused more on what seemed to be popular, profitable, and "disruptive" rather than on using the spiritual gifts God had entrusted to me.

During that season in business school, I began to take a hard look at who God had created me to be. To figure out which business God wanted me to start first, I started to ask soul-searching questions like,

- "What type of work gets me excited?"
- "What type of work am I good at?"
- "As I look back over my life, what type of work has God been preparing me to do?"
- "What are the things people say I do well?"

My responses to these clarifying questions led me to start a book publishing company. I had been an English major in college, taught academic writing to graduate students, edited numerous doctoral dissertations, and had written and published my own book. In addition, I enjoy marketing, had served as a marketing director, and had worked in direct sales.

Because it was an area in which I was gifted, starting a publishing company enabled me to launch a company immediately—without the need for investors or lenders. I got married in 2012, so I couldn't wait around for investors to start generating revenue from my business. I had to begin something immediately. My company cost very little to get started, and I was able to build it while working a full-time job in marketing. I started the company in 2013 with $100, and it now provides enough income for me to work from home, allow my wife to be a full-time mother for our young children, and fulfill my God-given calling at the same time.

The name of my publishing company, High Bridge Books, was inspired by the High Bridge, which connected my former neighborhood in Manhattan to the Bronx. Still the oldest bridge in New York City, it was built in 1848 as an aqueduct to provide water for the citizens of Manhattan. As the High Bridge provided life-sustaining water for the masses, High Bridge Books helps authors to provide life-changing books for the world. Through more than 25 books our authors have published since 2013, we have helped to make disciples of thousands of people, providing thought leadership for a variety of fields.

Our books are not necessarily Christian-themed books although they are consistent with what my authors and I consider to be a Christian worldview. Our books address topics such as leadership, marketing, education, abortion, religious freedom, motherhood, addiction recovery, adoption, and other topics that speak to specific human interests and issues in society. C.S. Lewis said, "What we want is not more little books about Christianity, but more little books by Christians on other subjects – with their Christianity latent."[1] As Lewis was implying, we do not need to sell Christian-themed products to make disciples through our commercial ventures.

The main way I make disciples through my business is through how I reveal the character of Jesus to my clients, customers, co-workers, and colleagues in the marketplace. This representation of Jesus is expressed primarily through my spiritual gifts, which are expressions and extensions of the Church—the Body of Christ—in the marketplace.

Why I Wrote This Book

Over the past few decades, many important books have been written about the problem of separating our "church life" from our "work life." I believe this Sunday-Monday gap is closing as Christians are understanding that the culture cannot be transformed merely from inside a church building. However, we need more practical marketplace ministry strategies for making this transformation happen.

My aim in writing this book is to equip you with a practical strategy for carrying out God's plan for revealing His glory, Jesus Christ, in the business world. As you journey through this book, my hope is that you will gain more clarity about your God-given, personalized ministry assignment in the marketplace.

Toward the end of this book, I have provided the *Spiritual Gifts in the Marketplace Assessment* to help you discover the unique abilities God has given to you for transforming the marketplace and making an eternal impact in your sphere of influence in business.

After you receive your assessment results, you can refer to the spiritual gift profiles for each of the 23 spiritual gifts evaluated in the assessment. Each profile includes a description of the gift, an example of how the gift has been used in a business setting, and references from the Bible to help you understand the biblical basis for each gift. Here are a few of the real-life examples of marketplace Christians using their spiritual gifts in business you will learn about:

- Cyber-security expert using the gift of discernment
- Business consultant using the gift of intercessory prayer
- Real estate developer using the gift of faith
- Professional athlete using the gift of healing

- Author using the gift of worship
- Department store owner using the gift of hospitality
- Venture capitalist using the gift of cross-cultural ministry
- Manufacturing company's CEO using the gift of compassion

Once you have identified your primary spiritual gifts, I encourage you to share with the *Theology of Business* community how you have used one or more of your spiritual gifts in a business setting. The links to share your examples are provided at the end of each spiritual gift profile.

Before we assess your personal spiritual gifts and how they can be used in a business setting, let's explore your broader assignment as a marketplace Christian.

---

[1] C.S. Lewis, *God in the Dock* (Grand Rapids: Eerdmans, 1970), 91.

PART 1

THE MARKETPLACE CHRISTIAN'S IDENTITY AND PURPOSE

Whatever you do, work at it with all your heart,
as working for the Lord, not for human masters, since you
know that you will receive an inheritance from the Lord
as a reward. It is the Lord Christ you are serving.

—COLOSSIANS 3:23-24

1

KINGS AND PRIESTS IN THE MARKETPLACE

IN MEETINGS WITH THE OPERATORS of his Chick-fil-a restaurants, CEO Dan Cathy asks these business leaders, "What are your career aspirations?" Inevitably, at least one of them will respond, "To be in full-time ministry." Many of these well-meaning marketplace Christians have been conditioned to believe that working in a local church or in a more traditional nonprofit ministry role would be more legitimate forms of Christian ministry than leading a for-profit business.

Dan Cathy takes these opportunities to explain that being a business leader is an important *ministry* role of the Church. (By the term, *Church*, I am referring to "the people of God"... not a building.) He tells them that the front counter at their Chick-fil-a restaurants is their "pulpit." He reminds them that the thousands of people who frequent their stores each week are their "congregations."

As a marketplace Christian, have you made the decision to be in "full-time ministry"? All it takes is a shift in purpose and motivation for doing business. As a born-again Christian, you already have the calling and all of the abilities necessary to be an effective marketplace minister.

Approximately 85 percent of the Christian workforce works in a for-profit company. Why is it that very few of these Christians seem to view themselves as being full-time ministers? When business professionals do not view their for-profit work as *ministry*, here are a few of the consequences:

- They assume God isn't relevant outside of church buildings.
- They don't read their Bibles, pray, or worship God outside of church services.
- They might view the Bible as containing "timeless business secrets" for succeeding in the marketplace and making money to fund "the Lord's work," but they aren't participating in God's plan for spreading the awareness of His glory in the marketplace.
- They don't actively share their faith or make disciples of Jesus.
- They don't hold themselves to the same standards of Christian conduct as those they consider to be "full-time ministers."
- They don't activate their spiritual gifts outside of volunteering through their local churches.

These Christians have been conditioned to think that *ministry* is supposed to happen only in church on Sunday, yet...

- Of Jesus' 132 public appearances in the New Testament, 122 were in the marketplace.

- Of 52 parables Jesus told, 45 had a workplace context.
- Of 40 divine interventions recorded in Acts, 39 occurred in the marketplace.[1]

There has been a general sense in institutional church culture that, if your salary isn't paid for by a Christian-themed organization (i.e. local church, missions board, parachurch ministry, etc.), you're just a "crowd Christian." Again, this is no small issue as about 85 percent of God's people in the developed world work in a for-profit company.

How did we get here?

More than Crowd Christians

Over many centuries, the institutional church unfortunately has invented, endorsed, and promoted a sharp division between what it has labeled the "clergy" and the "laity," or, "laymen." Having observed that this distinction did not emerge in the Church until the Third Century, Church historian Alexandre Faivre wrote,

> The layman is a strange being, subject to mutation, born the prisoner of an analogy, conditioned by a climate of the conflict and formed in a cultic environment.[2]

Let's unpack this statement.

Faivre said that the layman is a "strange being." That's because nobody knows what a *layman* is. We only know what a layman is not—that is, a Christian who doesn't get paid by a Christian-themed institution (e.g. local church, mission board, parachurch ministry, etc.). The term, *laity*, was invented by

Church leaders in approximately the Third Century not to identify what these people *were* but to identify what they *were not* (e.g. priests, deacons, bishops, etc.). The term comes from the Greek word, *laikos*, which means, "of the people." A layman was just a part of the crowd, a second-class outsider. Naturally, the term has become synonymous with ignorance (e.g. "the layman's guide," etc.).

Faivre said that the layman is "subject to mutation" because the roles of these Christians continues to be modified to suit the preferences of their pulpit ministers, not necessarily to activate their spiritual gifts and mobilize them for ministry among the extended Church in the marketplace. This is evident through the way many churches use spiritual gifts assessments with the primary purpose of finding places for their members to volunteer in church programs rather than to activate their spiritual gifts for ministry in the marketplace where they spend most of their waking hours.

When Faivre said, "born the prisoner of an analogy," he was referring to the Old Testament's Levitical priesthood model in which there were *priests...* and then... there was everyone else. Some prominent church leaders erroneously teach that there is still a spiritual "king and priest" distinction in the New Testament Church. In this separation, the pulpit ministers are considered the "priests" while the marketplace ministers are considered the "kings" that exist primarily to donate money to their "priests" (pastors) and "temples" (church buildings).

Marketplace Christians Are Royal Priests

Now that Jesus has made us "royal priests," this Levitical priesthood paradigm has shifted dramatically since the Old Testament (1 Pet. 2:9). As born-again Christians, we are all "royal priests" in the order of Jesus... not in the Levitical order of priests. Because Jesus is both the "King of Kings" and our "Great High Priest," God considers all born-again Christians as His "royal priests," for "as He is, so also are we in this world" (1 John 4:17, NASB). As marketplace ministers, we are not *either* kings *or* priests. We are, at once, kings and priests.

Being a royal priest may mean that you are supposed to volunteer at your local church for a few hours each week as a greeter, nursery worker, musician, usher, etc. At the same time, don't minimize your identity as a royal priest, which is who you are called to be seven days per week. You are not a junior royal priest, a second-tier royal priest, or a backup royal priest. You are the only royal priest many of the people in your workplace will encounter on a regular basis.

Now, let's discuss what it means to be "priests" and what it means to be "kings" in the marketplace.

Two Primary Duties of Priests in the Marketplace

There are two core functions of a royal priest, and approximately 85 percent of the Christian workforce is called to exercise these duties in a business setting.

Priest's Duty 1: **Sacrifice**

First, royal priests "offer spiritual sacrifices that please God" (1 Pet. 2:5b). As a marketplace Christian, what spiritual sacrifices have you made that please God?

Have you offered sacrifices of personal holiness in the marketplace through the way you live and conduct business? Those are spiritual sacrifices that please God.

Have you ever had to forgive someone in business? I'm sure you have... probably multiple times if you've been in the marketplace long enough. You may have had to forgive someone of a debt that had several zeros on the end of it. I know I have. Each time you forgive someone, especially when that forgiveness has zeroes on the end of it, you are making a sacrifice that pleases God as you reveal the merciful character of God Himself.

Have you sacrificed your financial earnings to God on a regular basis?

Have you ever had to sacrifice extra time at the office to spend time with your family?

Have you ever had to sacrifice selfish ambition for doing what God called you to do in business?

Your work itself should be a sacrificial offering to God. In fact, *work* (in its different forms) is mentioned more than 800 times in the Bible, more than all of the words used to express worship, music, praise, and singing combined.[3] When you do your work with excellence and for the glory of God, you are offering "spiritual sacrifices that please God."

Priest's Duty 2: **Proclaim**

The second duty of a royal priest is to "proclaim the excellencies of Him who has called you out of darkness into His marvelous light" (1 Peter 2:9b, NASB). In the Old Testament, the priests were responsible for going to God on behalf of the people. Then, they would go to the people on behalf of God, proclaiming His blessing and His goodness (see Num. 6:23-27).

D.L. Moody once said, "Of 100 men, one will read the Bible... the other 99 will read the Christian." As royal priests in the marketplace, we are called to "proclaim the excellencies" of Jesus in a business setting, sharing who He is, what He has done for us, and what He offers to humanity. This involves modeling and teaching the ways of God through how we conduct business.

Peter said, "If someone asks about your Christian hope, always be ready to explain it" (1 Pet. 3:15). The way in which we conduct ourselves in the marketplace should make people curious enough to ask us about our Christian hope. They might ask questions about our values, our behavior, our joy, our work ethic, or even our success. Ultimately, they are asking for a reason for the hope that we have: Jesus Christ. As priests in the marketplace, we are called to proclaim this hope.

Two Primary Duties of Kings in the Marketplace

Not only did God call us to enter His Kingdom, He called us to rule within His Kingdom. The first commandment given to humanity was to "fill the earth, and subdue it; and **rule**" (Gen. 1:28, NASB). We are called to "**reign** in life through the One, Jesus Christ" (Rom. 5:17, NASB).

As a marketplace Christian, you are a king, and a massive part of your domain is your sphere of influence in the marketplace. While our royal authority as children of God transcends the authorities among the kingdoms of the world, it should be revealed through our professional lives in the marketplace.

Let's explore two of our primary duties as God's appointed kings in the marketplace.

King's Duty 1: **Provide**

Kings have authority for the purpose of *providing* for those within their domains. As kings, what are some practical ways we can provide for the needs of those in our spheres of influence in the marketplace?

Provide your spiritual gifts – Whether your gifts are teaching, discernment, administration, prophecy, or any other, the marketplace needs your spiritual gifts. God's Word promises that He has made a place for our gifts (Prov. 18:16). It is our responsibility to make those gifts available in service to the world around us.

Be sure to take the *Spiritual Gifts in the Marketplace Assessment* in Part Three of this book to identify your own spiritual gifts. In Part Four, you will find profiles of 23 spiritual gifts that include examples of how each spiritual gift has been used in a business setting.

Provide economic value – If you are getting paid to do what you do, you most likely have provided an equivalent amount of economic value. In the process, you served at least one person by providing for at least one need.

Provide economic opportunities – Whether you have hired people or not, the economic value you provide for the marketplace creates opportunities for other people to contribute value. When one need is met, new needs emerge. The solution to one problem creates new problems to be solved.

Provide alms for the needy – Do you have co-workers who are hurting financially? If you are a business owner, do you have customers who can't pay? You may be the only one who knows about the impossible financial situations these people are in. Perhaps God is asking you to show mercy through providing some financial relief for that person.

As God's appointed king in the marketplace, how do you provide for the people within your sphere of influence?

King's Duty 2: **Protect**

Kings also are called to protect those within their domains. What are some practical ways we can protect those in our spheres of influence in the business world?

Protect through making wise and righteous decisions – Many of the decisions we make in business either will protect those in our spheres of influence, or they will hurt them. By making decisions in a way that protects those around us from financial, professional, emotional, relational, or even physical harm—rather than protecting our own selfish interests—we can serve our co-workers, customers, and colleagues with the servant's attitude of Jesus (Phil. 2:5).

Protect through life-giving words – On every economic level, the marketplace is extremely vulnerable to negativity and fear. Because of this, marketplace Christians have a significant opportunity and calling to protect those around us from this negativity and fear by speaking only "what is true, and honorable, and right, and pure, and lovely, and admirable… things that are excellent and worthy of praise" (Phil. 4:8).

Protect through prayer – Through our prayers, we can guard our companies against loss, theft, bad business partners, bad business deals, adverse market swings, and more. Many of these things are beyond our control, but they are not beyond the control and intervention of the Holy Spirit.

As a king, how is God asking you to protect those in your sphere of influence in the marketplace?

You Are Royalty

When Queen Victoria was a child, she didn't realize she was in line for the throne of England. Her instructors who were trying to prepare her for leadership were frustrated perpetually because they could not motivate young Victoria to take her schoolwork seriously.

Her instructors finally figured out she would not be able to lead others until she understood her identity. They admonished her, "One day, Victoria, you will be the Queen of England!"

Upon hearing this, Victoria said quietly, "Then, I will be good." The realization that she had inherited this high calling gave her a sense of authority, responsibility, and accountability that profoundly affected her conduct from that day forward.

Like Queen Victoria, we will always live in accordance with our understanding of who we are. As marketplace Christians, we are kings and priests who belong to God. This revelation will transform the business world as we walk in the fullness of our callings as marketplace Christians.

You are not merely a "layman," a crowd Christian. You are a priest called to offer spiritual sacrifices to God and to proclaim the hope and goodness of God to your co-workers, customers, vendors, bosses, board members, shareholders, and anyone else you encounter in the marketplace. You are also a king called to provide for and protect those within your sphere of influence in business. You are a frontline Christian, a marketplace minister. If you are called to the marketplace, do not wish you were the leader of a Christian-themed nonprofit organization. As a marketplace Christian, you are hereby "in the ministry." God has called you to represent Him right where you are in business.

Group Discussion: Are you fulfilling all of your duties as both a king and priest in the marketplace? In which of the four duties do you need to improve the most?

---

[1] Os Hillman, *The 9 to 5 Window* (Ventura California: Regal Books, 2005), 23.

[2] Alexandre Faivre, *The Emergence of the Laity in the Early Church*, Trans. David Smith (New York: Paulist Press, 1990), 21.

[3] Os Hillman, "Faith & Work Fact Sheet", http://www.marketplaceleaders.org/faith-work-factsheet/.

2

THE MARKETPLACE NEEDS CHRISTIANS

THE APOSTLE PAUL IS CREDITED with writing 14 of the 27 books in the New Testament, and he is considered one of the most influential people in the history of the world. At the same time, he was a business professional who made tents for a living.

Like other Jewish males, Paul would have been taught a particular trade as a boy—such as tent-making—and he also would have been taught how to make money with it. Because tents were used primarily to provide housing for soldiers, it is likely that the Roman army was Paul's largest customer during his stay in Corinth. His customers also may have included the tourists who traveled to Corinth to watch the Isthmian Games.

Paul did not abandon the marketplace when he started serving Jesus. Instead, his entrepreneurial, tent-making enterprise served as a key element of his apostolic ministry. Referring to his profit-generating endeavors, Paul told the Thessalonians to "follow our example" (2 Thess. 3:7). He said that it is "a model for you" (2 Thess. 3:9).

Why did Paul include this "example" and "model" of for-profit enterprise as a key aspect of his ministry? Why is the marketplace an ideal ministry environment for most Christians to exercise their spiritual gifts? Let's explore nine reasons why the marketplace is a great place for Christians.

Reason 1: Almost all non-Christians are in the marketplace.

Today, less than 20 percent of people in the United States attend church regularly—"regular" church attendance being defined as attending church services at least two times per month. In many European countries, the percentages are much lower. At the current rate, regular church attendance in the U.S. is projected to drop to 11.7 percent by 2050.[1]

The good news is that these people who do not attend local church services still will be waking up to go to work alongside their Christian co-workers in the marketplace each week.

Reason 2: It's easier to understand and relate to the culture in the marketplace.

Paul was called by God to minister primarily to the Gentiles in the Greco-Roman world—not primarily to the Jews in the Jewish world. Although the Jewish people were familiar with the Old Testament law that the Levitical priests were entitled to live off of the donations given by those who worked outside of the temple, this Jewish cultural practice would have been more difficult for the Gentiles of the Greco-Roman world to accept.

I believe this cultural difference is one reason why Paul chose to pay himself primarily from his own business rather than to live off of donations from the churches where he preached. Paul explained, "When I preach the gospel, I may offer the gospel without charge, so as not to make full use of my right in the gospel" (1 Cor. 9:18). Adapting to the Greco-Roman culture in this way is an example of how Paul accomplished his objective to "become all things to all men, so that I may by all means save some" (1 Cor. 9:22). [Yes, when Paul was locked up in the jail, he did accept donations to help with meeting his needs, presumably because it would have been difficult to build his business from jail (Phil. 4:18).]

The cultural expectation that pulpit ministers remain financially self-sufficient—often referred to as "tent-making"—remains deeply ingrained in today's Greek churches. Especially considering the weak economy in Greece today, most Greek churches are not in a financial position to pay their leaders' salaries. I know a Greek pastor in Thessaloniki who shares the leadership of his church with three other men as he works three different jobs to support his family.

Culturally, today's Western society is much more like the first-century Greco-Roman world than the first-century Jewish world. The typical unchurched business professional in the United States simply cannot relate to living off of donations. Because of this cultural dynamic, Christian business professionals are in a great position to minister to other business professionals in a relevant way in the marketplace. Our needs are met by the compensation we receive for the value we create in the marketplace, so we can use our spiritual gifts free-of-charge to advance the gospel and reveal the glory of God.

Reason 3: Almost all Christians work in the marketplace.

At least 85 percent of the Christian workforce spends 60-70 percent of their waking hours in the marketplace. Most of us spend more of our waking hours at work than at home.

Because of this reality, in addition to serving our families and volunteering with our local churches, the marketplace may be our greatest opportunity for using our spiritual gifts to spread the awareness of God's glory. The potential eternal impact for Christians ministering with our spiritual gifts collaboratively in the marketplace is limitless!

Reason 4: The marketplace provides more discipleship opportunities.

Pulpit ministers often are criticized for the lack of discipleship and spiritual growth among their congregations. Let's give our pulpit ministers a break. Certainly, lives are touched by the Holy Spirit on Sunday morning in church buildings all over the world. But how much *discipleship* actually can happen during a two-hour church service on four Sundays out of each month?

Discipleship—that is, becoming more like Jesus—happens through relationships in everyday life. I believe that is why, of Jesus' 132 public appearances in the New Testament, 122 were in the marketplace. Also, of 52 parables Jesus told, 45 had a workplace context. Yes, discipleship can happen anywhere; however, the potential for discipleship impact during a weekly church service is a fraction of what is possible during an entire work-week spent with our co-workers, clients, customers, and colleagues in business.

Reason 5: The marketplace is an authentic showroom of Christianity.

If you were shopping for a car, you probably would go to a showroom or a car lot. Before you bought anything, you probably would want to see if the car actually functioned properly on the road. You might even ask the dealer to allow you to take the car home for a day or two to test it out.

Using this metaphor, if unbelievers are the *customers* of Christianity, the local church is the *showroom*, and the marketplace is the *test drive*. The marketplace is where our unbelieving co-workers and customers get to see if they really want what we have. Daily, they see how we react under pressure. They see how we treat people. They see how much God truly matters—or doesn't matter—to us in our daily lives.

Reason 6: The marketplace provides opportunities for all of the Church's spiritual gifts to be used.

Our local churches usually cannot deliberately facilitate enough opportunities for everyone in the church to use their spiritual gifts in the church building. Usually, the "service" aspect of Sunday morning services revolves around the pastor's preaching gift and the musicians' gifts of worship and creativity. Some members of the congregation may volunteer occasionally as nursery workers, front door greeters, parking lot attendants, etc. However, the majority of the spiritual gifts in our local church congregations remains relatively untapped by local church programs.

At the same time, the Christian life cannot fully make sense until we are using our spiritual gifts toward fulfilling the mission of the Church in the world. Although local churches do provide some ministry opportunities for their congregations, for most of us, our spiritual gifts are intended to be used primarily in the marketplace. That's where most of us spend the majority of our waking hours each week.

Reason 7: Denominational divisions are less stifling in the marketplace.

We can choose whether to attend a Baptist, Pentecostal-Charismatic, Presbyterian, Non-Denominational Church, etc... but most of us do not have the luxury of co-working only with Christians with whom we agree theologically. The marketplace has a way of diluting some of these differences. This opens the door to collaborative ministry beyond the walls of our local churches and liturgical traditions. If we will allow it, the denominational diversity of the Church in the marketplace can create a unified, compound effect of Kingdom impact in the culture.

Reason 8: Everything gets funded from the marketplace.

In addition to providing for his own financial needs, Paul the Apostle used his tent-making enterprise to provide a means for his team members to generate income. Paul wrote,

> You yourselves know that **these hands ministered to my own needs and to the men who were with me**. In everything I showed you that by working hard **in this manner** you must help the weak and remember the words of the Lord Jesus, that He Himself said, "It is more blessed to give than to receive." (Acts 20:33-35, NASB)

In the passage above, Paul was explaining that working hard in the marketplace enabled him to financially support, not only himself and his ministry team, but also the poor.

All money comes from value that has been created in the marketplace, and business professionals ultimately decide what gets funded. Business professionals create tremendous value, which provides us with the potential for tremendous generosity toward other expressions of the Lord's work beyond our personal marketplace ministry assignments. As business professionals, we must seek to know God and His plan for our lives in order to make righteous decisions concerning money.

Reason 9: The marketplace provides a context for teaching personal discipline to our fellow Christians.

Many of the Thessalonians to whom Paul preached assumed that the imminent Second Coming of Jesus Christ gave them a legitimate excuse to be lazy and abandon their responsibilities in the marketplace. They thought, *Jesus is coming back soon, so we don't need to worry about "worldly" and "temporary" things such as business.* This misguided theology provided inspiration for Paul's famous words, "If anyone is not willing to work, then he is not to eat, either" (2 Thess. 3:10). Paul tore through the Thessalonians excuses for not doing business by exhorting them to "follow our example" of working hard in business to demonstrate the gospel through their disciplined lifestyles (2 Thess. 3:7, 9).

As a marketplace Christian, you are an example of personal discipline to many people around you. Use this earned authority as an opportunity to inspire people to use their own spiritual gifts for ministry in the marketplace.

Group Discussion: Which of these nine reasons stands out to you the most? Why is God aggressively mobilizing Christian business professionals for ministry in the marketplace today?

---

1 Kelly Shattuck, "7 Startling Facts: An Up Close Look at Church Attendance in America," *ChurchLeaders.com*, http://www.churchleaders.com/pastors/pastor-articles/139575-7-startling-facts-an-up-close-look-at-church-attendance-in-america.html.

3

MYTHS ABOUT OUR PRIMARY MISSION IN THE MARKETPLACE

THE CHURCH HAS COME A LONG WAY in the past few decades toward mobilizing Christians for ministry in the marketplace. At the same time, the truth about ministry in the marketplace has been hiding behind a few myths that are hindering today's Marketplace Transformation Movement. Here are a few of those myths about the primary mission of marketplace Christians:

Myth 1: "It's mainly about applying timeless business principles."

The Bible is full of practical business wisdom that has proven effective in the marketplace since the creation of economics and the marketplace in the Garden of Eden. For example, the *Book of Proverbs* is filled with timeless wisdom about business issues such as finance, wise counsel, leadership, integrity, and much more. In fact, I love the *Book of Proverbs* so much that I named my firstborn son Solomon!

I even wrote a book about 25 marketing strategies and principles I observed from the life and ministry of Jesus. Regardless of your religious affiliation, you can apply the strategies from *Marketing Like Jesus* in your own business and experience tremendous success! I love the timeless business wisdom found in the Bible!

Christians and non-Christians alike can apply the Bible's timeless business principles and experience the benefits. Therefore, it's possible to apply and benefit from the business principles found in the Bible while never really knowing the God who established those principles. With only a set of timeless principles, we are left with only rules but no relationship. God is a person, not merely a set of timeless principles. With only a set of timeless principles, we are left only with ethics and no purpose to undergird and fuel those ethics.

Our primary mission in the marketplace must be about more than applying Biblical business principles.

Myth 2: "It's mainly about being financially prosperous."

The Bible says, "Wealth is a blessing of the Lord, and He adds no sorrow to it" (Prov. 10:22). We are admonished, "Remember the Lord your God, for it is he who gives you *the ability to produce wealth*, and so confirms his covenant, which he swore to your forefathers, as it is today" (Deut. 8:18). Although financial wealth comes from God, the attainment of financial wealth is not our primary purpose as marketplace Christians.

Some have taken verses like Deuteronomy 8:18 and Proverbs 10:22 to support a theology that one's spirituality and faith can be judged on the basis of how much money he or she has. The truth is that one's ability to gain money and influence is not necessarily determined by whether his or her motives and methods are pure.

Many businesses led by non-Christians are on the *Fortune 500, Inc. 500,* and other lists of the most successful companies in the world. Many of the *"Forbes* 400 Richest People in the World" are not followers of Jesus. Jesus explained this phenomenon when he said God "causes His sun to rise on the evil and the good, and sends rain on the righteous and the unrighteous" (Matt. 5:45b).

Although creating value and rendering high-quality service in the marketplace will produce profit, Jesus never taught us to pursue material wealth. Because of this, the pursuit of financial prosperity should not be our primary aim as marketplace Christians, and it should not serve as a basis on which we evaluate the power of our faith.

True prosperity, which endures in eternity, comes from spreading the awareness of God's glory. As we pursue Jesus and spread the awareness of his glory in the marketplace, all of our needs will be met, and we will have plenty left over to meet others' needs.

Myth 3: "It's mainly about being able to give away more money."

I have found that many marketplace Christians view "offering time" on Sunday morning as their primary ministry through the Church, failing to use the full range of their spiritual gifts for the glory of God in the marketplace. Many marketplace Christians even feel that their spirituality is being judged on the basis of how much money they produce and put into the offering plate.

Certainly, God created us to create and give, and we are stewards of our God-given power to produce and share wealth. However, giving financially to our local churches is only one expression of our worship to God, and the spiritual gift of *giving* is only one of the spiritual gifts. It is just as important as the other spiritual gifts.

Myth 4: "It's mainly about inventing new ways of 'doing church.'"

Using spiritual gifts in the marketplace is not about transplanting local church service models into a business setting. It's not about packing your co-workers into the conference room, playing worship music, and bringing in your pastor to preach to them. (Although that would be awesome if God arranged that!)

Marketplace ministry is not a substitute for the local church. It is an expression and outreach of the local church. Your spiritual gifts are extensions of your local church. Although you use them in the marketplace, they are contributions to the mission of your local church and the universal Church of Jesus Christ.

Myth 5: "It's mainly about selling Christian-themed stuff to Christian people."

I have noticed that many Christians who sense God calling them to do business as a form of ministry assume this means selling Christian-themed stuff to Christian people (i.e. Christian-themed coffee shops, books, music, t-shirts, memberships, etc.). This approach is simply one marketing model, and it is not necessarily more or less righteous than any other marketing model. In most parts of the world, people who identify as Christians represent a massive percentage of the population, so it makes good business sense to have Christ-centered companies serving an explicitly "Christian" market by providing Christian-themed goods and services. In fact, the book you are reading now is Christian-themed.

At the same time, we are called to disciple entire industries. This will require that we, as Christians in the marketplace, set our sights on broader market shares than merely those that are explicitly Christian-themed.

Myth 6: "It should look the same for all marketplace Christians."

If my primary spiritual gifts are pastoring or compassion, I probably am going to view ministry in the marketplace as a calling to "care for the personal needs of my employees and/or co-workers" (e.g. marketplace chaplains).

If my primary gift as a marketplace Christian is apostleship, it is likely that I will view ministry in the marketplace as a mandate to "walk in my God-given authority and dominion" in the marketplace (e.g. "The 7 Mountains Mandate").

If I have the spiritual gift of evangelism as a marketplace Christian, I probably will be more inclined than most other marketplace Christians to evangelize in my workplace. (Or, as human resources departments like to refer to it… "proselytize.")

As we make the shift toward using our spiritual gifts in the marketplace, we must tap into our own God-given spiritual gifts rather than wishing we had someone else's. We also must avoid the trap of projecting our gifts onto others, expecting them to approach marketplace ministry with the same methods we use. The "one-size-fits-all" approach only produces self-condemnation and ineffectiveness for marketplace Christians attempting to operate outside of their God-given spiritual gifts.

As marketplace ministers, all of our spiritual gifts are necessary for fulfilling the Great Commission in the marketplace. By the time you finish reading this book, my prayer is that you will have a working knowledge of your own God-given spiritual gifts and a framework for how to use them in your own sphere of influence in the marketplace.

Group Discussion: Which of these six "myths" about our primary mission in the marketplace stands out to you the most?

4

MAKING YOUR INDUSTRY A DISCIPLE OF JESUS

HABBAKUK PROPHESIED, "For as the waters fill the sea, the earth will be filled with an awareness of the glory of the Lord" (Hab. 2:14). What is the "glory of the Lord" that will fill the whole earth, including the marketplace? The Hebrew word for *glory, kavod,* means, "weightiness." God's glory is weighty. It matters more than all things, whether people realize its weightiness or not. Glory neither can be given to God nor taken away from Him. It already belongs to Him. In business or in any other facet of culture, nothing matters more nor is anything more "weighty" than God.

Notice Habbakuk did not prophesy that the earth will *eventually* be filled with the glory of God. This is because the earth is already filled with His glory. His glory is not lacking. Currently, the world's "awareness" of His glory is what is lacking. That is why Habbakuk prophesied that "the earth will be filled with an *awareness* of the glory of the Lord." As marketplace ministers, then, our mission is to make the marketplace *aware* of His glory.

More specifically, what is God's "glory"? The writer of Hebrews said, "The Son is the radiance of God's glory and the exact representation of his being" (Heb. 1:3). There is our answer: *Jesus Christ* is the glory of God. The whole earth, including the marketplace, will become aware of the glory of the Lord that is Jesus Christ. So, we can interpret Habbakuk 2:14 as follows:

> For as the waters fill the sea, the earth [including the marketplace] will be filled with an awareness of the glory of God [Jesus Christ].

As marketplace ministers, we are called to spread the awareness of God's glory, Jesus Christ. This is the Great Commission Jesus gave to his disciples. He commissioned us to "make disciples of *all nations*" (Matt. 28:19). In other words, the glory of God is to be revealed throughout the whole earth, not to individuals only. We are called to help individuals, communities, nations, and even industries to reveal the glorious image of Jesus. The more we become *aware* of Jesus, the more we will *reveal* His image to the world around us. The same applies for nations and industries. As we spread the awareness of His glory, God will cause His glory to be represented through that person, nation, or industry. Jesus is the embodiment of God's Kingdom, His rule and reign. His glory. His weightiness. God wants His Kingdom to be revealed through us "on earth as it is in heaven" (Matt. 6:10).

In business or in any other facet of culture, nothing matters more than Jesus, the glory of God. We are the ones God wants to use to spread the awareness that He matters more than anything in every place. God is relevant everywhere, not just at church on Sunday morning.

Johann Sebastian Bach, the 18th century German musician, finished many of his compositions with the initials, "S.D.G." These initials stood for "Soli Deo gloria," meaning "Glory to

God alone." He believed that the only work that matters is work done to spread the awareness of God's glory. Bach wrote, "The aim and final end of all music should be none other than the glory of God and the refreshment of the soul." Likewise, this should be the attitude that drives all of our work in the marketplace.

The Discipleship of Industries

Because of sin, God's creation is presently in decay and darkness. Until the "awareness" of the glory of God, Jesus Christ, shines into the marketplace, it will remain in bondage to sin and all of its nasty expressions: corruption, greed, poverty, selfish ambition, pride, godlessness, spiritual emptiness, depression, and much more.

That's where marketplace ministers come in. Jesus instructed us that we are to spread the awareness of God's glory by being "salt" and "light" to triumph over the decay and darkness in our fallen world (Matt. 5:13-14). In addition to seeing individuals set free from the power of sin, it is God's will that *all* of creation would be set free. The revelation of God's glory, Jesus Christ, enables our spheres of influence in the marketplace to become free from the curse of sin. As we fulfill our callings to be salt and light in the marketplace,

> ...the creation itself also will be set free from its slavery to corruption into the freedom of the glory of the children of God. (Rom. 8:21, NASB)

The opportunity we have to transform the marketplace through revealing Jesus is a foreshadowing of God's "final restoration of all things as God promised long ago through his holy prophets" (Acts 3:21). In the meantime, Jesus has given to us the charge of fulfilling the will of God "on earth as it is in heaven" (Matt. 6:10).

We cannot fulfill our mandate to disciple nations without discipling the marketplace. More specifically, we must disciple our own spheres of influence in the marketplace—that is, our respective industries. Business industries wield more control over the direction and definition of a nation than any other facet of culture.

Your industry is already being discipled by somebody.

If we do not disciple our industries, they will be discipled by people who have godless value systems. In fact, people already are discipling our industries in one direction or another, either leading them toward the awareness of the glory of God or in the pursuit of a counterfeit glory. This is especially true in the United States and Europe where the religion of Secular Humanism currently dominates many industries. Secular Humanism attempts to rob God of his glory with cleverly-marketed, godless worldviews. It attempts to usurp the Lordship of Jesus Christ over the marketplace by leading people in the pursuit of a false glory.

Consider the film industry. Although the Academy Awards ceremony, "The Oscars," is usually an entertaining show for any movie-goer, the ceremony does not exist primarily for the enjoyment of movie-goers. Rather, it is an annual opportunity for the members of the film industry to honor those among their peers who they feel have made the greatest contributions to their industry. Each Academy Award nomination defines the culture of the film industry, which then affects the broader cultures of the nations in which those films are watched.

How would you describe the prevailing culture of your industry? In other words...

- How are Christians viewed?
- What are the worldviews of the industry's leaders?
- What are the ethical norms?
- What gets celebrated in your industry?
- How are the customers treated?
- How is your industry perceived by the public?
- What are the dominant beliefs concerning politics, religion, etc.?

Are you actively shaping the culture of your industry? In other words, how are you helping your industry to reveal the glorious image of Jesus Christ?

Challenging Secular Humanism in the Marketplace

Legendary Christian author, C.S. Lewis, has provided an outstanding model of how to disciple an industry while allowing the fullest expression of his personal faith and identity. *The Times*, which is the main British national daily newspaper, ranked Lewis 11th on its list of "The 50 Greatest British Writers since 1945."[1] He wrote books explicitly for a Christian audience while writing others—notably, the *Chronicles of Narnia* series—for a general audience. Explaining how his industry, book publishing, could be used for the "re-conversion" of the entire nation of England, C.S. Lewis wrote in his book, *God in the Dock*,

We must attack the enemy's line of communication. What we want is not more little books about Christianity, but more little books by Christians on other subjects—with their Christianity latent. You can see this most easily if you look at it the other way around. Our Faith is not very likely to be shaken by any book on Hinduism. But if whenever we read an elementary book on Geology, Botany, Politics, or Astronomy, we found that its implications were Hindu, that would shake us. It is not the books written in direct defense of Materialism that make the modern man a materialist; it is the materialistic assumptions in all the other books. In the same way, it is not books on Christianity that will really trouble him. But he would be troubled if, whenever he wanted a cheap popular introduction to some science, the best work on the market was always by a Christian. The first step to the re-conversion of this country is a series, produced by Christians, which can beat the Penguin and the Thinkers Library on their own ground. Its Christianity would have to be latent, not explicit: and of course its science perfectly honest. Science twisted in the interests of apologetics would be sin and folly.[2]

Let's unpack this passage.

Lewis stated, "We must attack the enemy's line of communication." He recognized that Satan has been using Secular Humanism, a godless worldview under the guise of a non-religion, as a primary tool for leading people and cultures away from God. Secular Humanists organize and operate as dogmatic disciples of their religion—that is, the worship of one's self—without the stigma of being known as followers of a "religion." Because most of the world's major religions inhibit them from expressing this worship of themselves, they preach that *religion* is the problem. Preaching the separation of Church and everything, they have been free to infiltrate and indoctrinate the major spheres of influence in society with their religion: Family, Business, Government, Entertainment, Media, Religion, and Education. When they preach that God is irrelevant, unimportant, and even counterproductive in these spheres of influence, what they mean is that worshipping God inhibits their freedom to express the worship of themselves.

In every sphere of cultural influence, Lewis wanted Christians to challenge the weak foundation, inconsistencies, deceit, and selfish agendas of Secular Humanists lest Christians continue to be marginalized in Western society.

Lewis' statement about keeping our Christianity "latent" has been taken out of context many times. I have seen it used several times as an excuse for Christians to be undifferentiated and lukewarm among nonbelievers in the culture. When Lewis spoke of the need for "latent" Christianity, he was not encouraging Christians to put the light of the world, the glory of God, "under a basket" so that it would be hidden from the world (Matt. 5:15). As we have explored already in this chapter, just the opposite is true.

As we read C.S. Lewis' entire passage above, we understand that "latent" Christianity was part of his strategy for the "reconversion of this country [England]." In other words, he wanted to see his entire nation become a disciple of Jesus through Christians influencing from the tops of their fields and industries, not only from Christian-themed fields and niche sub-industries.

Lewis envisioned a day in his industry, book publishing, when "the best work on the market was always by a Christian."

For Lewis, this vision of discipling an entire nation could not be realized only by marketing explicitly Christian ideas, products, and services to Christian people. It would require Christians to create and market outstanding ideas, products, and services—built on their Christian faith and expressed through their spiritual gifts—that would cause them to rise to high positions of influence in their respective fields and industries. That is why he admonished Christians by saying, "What we want is not more little books about Christianity, but more little books by Christians on other subjects."

Most pulpit ministers have the calling and freedom to be explicit about their faith because they almost always are ministering to a captive audience of like-minded believers in a religious setting.

Most marketplace ministers, on the other hand, are called to more "latent" and covert expressions of our faith because we almost always are ministering to unbelievers in a marketplace setting.

Jesus said, "The Kingdom of Heaven is like the yeast a woman used in making bread. Even though she put only a little yeast in three measures of flour, it permeated every part of the dough" (Matt. 13:33). We are called to be the "yeast" that permeates and transforms the world from the inside out.

Group Discussion: What would it look like if your entire industry reflected the glory of God? Is it possible?

---

[1] "The 50 greatest British writers since 1945," *The Times* (January 5, 2008).

[2] C.S. Lewis, *God in the Dock* (Grand Rapids: Eerdmans, 1970), 91.

5

Identifying Your God-Given Marketplace Assignment

As MARKETPLACE CHRISTIANS, we are called to help the marketplace to reveal the glory of God, beginning with the industries to which God has called each of us. You now may be wondering, "To what industry has God called *me*?"

Now that we have clarified the primary purpose of our work in the marketplace, let's explore three criteria we can use to identify the specific industries to which God has assigned each of us. These are the industries to which God has called us to use our spiritual gifts for ministry as extensions of the Church in the marketplace.

1: It's an industry whose mission you're *passionate* about.

When I was in business school, I attempted to start a website that would be a "one-stop shop for purchasing fitness services" (e.g. gym memberships, exercise classes, etc.). I lost $5,000 in the process by paying a poorly vetted and untrustworthy web developer to build the prototype of the website.

As soon as I lost that money, I decided to learn how to build the website myself. As I started to list the various fitness service providers on the website, I quickly realized that I was not as passionate about the fitness industry as I thought I was. Or, at least, I did not enjoy the industry enough to build a company in it. Although I exercise six days out of most weeks and had been studying the fitness industry rigorously throughout the year prior, only when I started working in the industry did I realize it was not the "right fit" for me.

Primed and ready to start a company, I asked myself, "Which industry's mission *am* I passionate about?" My answer came back almost immediately: the publishing industry, whose mission is to help people by sharing literature and information online and offline (i.e. books, podcasts, blogs, courses, etc.). I love books, learning, and teaching. This was an important clue about my industry calling. Working with authors and books is wonderfully fulfilling for me.

God wants us to be fulfilled in our work. King Solomon wrote, "I have seen that nothing is better than that man should be happy in his activities, for that is his lot" (Ecc. 3:22).

What is the mission of the industry you are working in currently? Gain clarity about that. In the publishing industry, it would be foolish for a printing company owner to assume printing is the core mission of the publishing industry. No, it's about publishing information, which increasingly is happening digitally rather than through print... as many newspapers, magazines, and book publishing companies now are finding out the hard way. Printing is one part of the publishing industry.

Once you have identified the core mission of your industry, ask yourself, "Am I passionate about this mission?"

As an example, if you work for an airline company, you are in the transportation industry, whose mission is to move people and things where they need to go. Are you passionate about improving people's lives by providing this type of service? If not, you're probably in the wrong industry.

2: It's an industry you have *experience* in.

Discovering my calling to the publishing industry came through reflecting on my past professional experiences. I considered that I already had published a book, majored in English in college, taught writing at the university level, edited several doctoral dissertations, and served as a marketing director. With these experiences, I was prepared to make an impact in an industry focused on publishing, distributing, and marketing information.

While I was majoring in English in college, I had no idea how to answer people when they started asking me, "What are you going to do with that English degree?" Now, I realize that God was using that experience to prepare me to start a publishing company.

In many cases, God has allowed us to have these past experiences to equip us for and lead us into the industry He has called us to transform for His glory. The Bible says, "And we know that God causes everything to work together for the good of those who love God and are called according to his purpose for them" (Rom. 8:28). "All things" includes *all* of our past professional experiences.

In what industries do you have experience?

As I discovered, the only way to verify that you are truly passionate about the core mission of an industry is to gain experience in that industry. If you think God might be prompting you to explore a new industry, it could be the next step toward identifying the industry to which He has called you.

3: It's an industry in which you can create *economic value*.

Two of my top three spiritual gifts are knowledge and teaching. The books published by my company, High Bridge Books, are inherently teaching and knowledge tools for which people pay money. The primary way I use my gifts of teaching and knowledge is through coaching authors, helping them to craft and spread their messages in the most effective ways possible.

My spiritual gifts certainly are in great demand in the publishing industry, which enables me to create economic value, make money, and make an eternal impact daily.

Without a doubt, your spiritual gifts are also in demand in the industry to which God has assigned you.

Group Discussion: What industry has God called you to transform for His glory?

6

TRANSFORMING YOUR INDUSTRY FOR THE GLORY OF GOD

IT'S TIME TO GET MORE PRACTICAL AND TACTICAL about helping the marketplace to become aware of and ultimately to reveal the glory of God. Here are seven strategies to transform your industry for the glory of God.

1: Focus on a niche sub-industry.

A niche sub-industry is a specific sphere of influence in which you can meet a specific need in your market by delivering a specific type of economic value to a specific group of people. As an example, when an actor succeeds in a specific genre of films, the actor can begin to appear in and influence other genres of films.

Often, those of us who sense God calling us to disciple nations through transforming cultures have a hard time starting small. We understand God has called us to "make disciples of all nations," but it is difficult for many of us to understand that beginning with a target group of people is a key strategy required for fulfilling this Great Commission. God is calling each of us to fulfill the Great Commission in a specific area and among a specific group of people. For Christians in the marketplace, this means selecting an industry and helping that industry and the people in it to reveal the glory of God.

As I explained in my book, *Marketing Like Jesus: 25 Strategies to Change the World*, while Jesus' mission was to reach the entire world with his message, He first focused on serving a specific group of people during the three years of his ministry on earth: the Jewish people. The Apostle Paul explained that Jesus' message came to the Jewish people first:

> For I am not ashamed of the gospel, for it is the power of God for salvation to everyone who believes, to the Jew *first* and also to the Greek. (Romans 1:16, emphasis mine)

When a non-Jewish woman asked Jesus to heal her demon-possessed daughter, Jesus responded, "I was sent only to the lost sheep of *the house of Israel*" (Matthew 15:24, emphasis mine). Though Jesus had compassion on this Gentile woman and served her, he reminded her that she was not part of his target group. When she implored him to help her and her daughter, Jesus said, "It is not good to take the children's bread and throw it to the dogs" (Matt. 15:26). The Samaritan woman understood that the gospel message was ultimately for everybody, but she also understood that Jesus was focused primarily on sharing his message with the Jewish people during his time of personal ministry. Seeing she understood that the gospel was for everyone in the world, Jesus responded, "O woman, your faith is great; it shall be done for you as you wish" (Matt. 15:28).

Not only did Jesus target his message toward a specific ethnic group and nationality, the Jewish people in Israel, he targeted a specific subgroup among the Jewish people: the outcasts. Jesus said of his ministry on earth, "I have come to the *lost sheep* of the house of Israel" (Matt. 15:24, emphasis mine). These "lost sheep" were the despised and outcast members of Israel's society: "the tax collectors and the sinners." The Bible says, "There were many people of this kind among Jesus' followers" (Mark 2:15b). Everything he said and did was said and done with this specific group in mind. During his public ministry, Jesus did not target Israel's best and brightest. He did not go after the pillars of the community. Wayward as they were, he targeted the "disreputable sinners" that epitomized the "lost sheep of the house of Israel." Insignificant as they were, these "lost sheep" were the ones who spread Jesus' message around the world.

After you have identified the industry you are called to disciple, you need to select a sub-industry, niche, genre, or sub-genre within that industry. As a book publisher, I have worked with many authors who were, at first, afraid to target their messages toward a specific target group. Many of us fear that we would be "limiting" our impact by targeting a specific group. After all, wouldn't we reach a larger audience if we try to reach "everybody"? No, that's a myth. Ironically, products and services that are marketed to "everybody" usually reach very few people.

First of all, not everybody wants what an individual person is offering. Second, an individual will not have the resources to reach "everybody"—at least, not initially.

Yes, have a massive vision, but also aim for a small target within the scope of your overall vision. Zig Ziglar said, "If you aim at nothing, you will hit it everytime." To disciple an entire industry, start with a niche sub-industry.

2: Set an example worth following.

Making disciples of Jesus in a business setting may sound more complicated than it is. The Apostle Paul simplified and defined disciple-making with this invitation: "Imitate me as I imitate Christ" (1 Cor. 11:1).

Does the way you do business reveal Jesus Christ, the glory of God? In other words, do you treat your employees, customers, clients, and other stakeholders as Jesus would? Like the Apostle Paul, have you invited others to follow your example? If so, you are making disciples, followers of Jesus. It's that simple.

3: Apply your spiritual gifts in your industry.

Your industry needs your spiritual gifts. Your spiritual gifts are channels for the supernatural power of God, which is essential for spreading the awareness of Jesus in your industry. This is how lasting change can happen, not merely the flaky kind that went "viral" on the internet last year yet is now forgotten.

A Christian business professional named Paul uses his gift of discernment in the information security industry by helping businesses and government agencies solve difficult security challenges. Over the years, his supernatural effectiveness in profiling people and solving complex problems has caused multiple business leaders and government employees to ask him, "What's your secret?" When Paul was asked this question at the end of a training class he led for an agency of the United States intelligence community, he responded, "I am a servant of the most high God..." In front of a room full of elite government agents, he then shared his faith in God.

Paul then explained to the audience how the Holy Spirit gives various spiritual gifts to those who are sons and daughters of God and have sought the Holy Spirit and His gifts. He shared that one of his primary spiritual gifts is discernment, which helps him to glorify God through upholding justice as an information security expert and practitioner.

After he finished, the entire room erupted in applause due to Paul's boldness in sharing his beliefs. Afterward, individual agents came to him personally to ask more questions about his faith.

4: Align your spiritual gifts with your role in the marketplace.

Sadly, many people are in marketplace roles for which they have not been gifted by the Holy Spirit. If this sounds like you, it may be the season for a change. Fortunately, your spiritual gifts are in demand in your current industry, and they are transferrable into almost any industry.

For example, let's say you love music, and you want to be in the music industry. This does not necessarily mean you should become a recording artist. One of your dominant gifts may be the gift of administration. If that's the case, you probably will be most effective in transforming the music industry if you are working in an administrative role within the music industry.

Do not despise the potential impact that can be made by your spiritual gifts in your industry. Your role is vital to the disciple-making operation of the Church in the marketplace.

5: Love your industry.

Do you love your industry? The Apostle Paul wrote, "If I have the gift of prophecy, and know all mysteries and all knowledge; and if I have all faith, so as to remove mountains, but do not have love, I am nothing" (1 Cor. 13:2). Our spiritual gifts are useless for changing our industries for the glory of God unless they are motivated by love for the people who work within them.

Here are a few ways you can love your industry:

- **Pray for those operating within your industry.** (Includes praying for your competitors)
- **Speak life-giving words about your industry.** (Includes what you say about your competitors)
- **Learn all you can about your industry.** (Who are the thought leaders in your industry that you need to follow?)
- **Make your spiritual gifts fully available to the work of the Holy Spirit in your industry.** (Do not reserve them only for use within the four walls of your local church. Remember, your spiritual gifts are extensions of your local church into the marketplace.)
- **Innovate and challenge your industry to improve to create more value and to serve people better.** (Those of us who work for Jesus and through the power of the Holy Spirit should cause our industries to achieve high levels of excellence.)

6: Get your business advice primarily from fellow Christians.

There are many thought leaders in and around my industry that I respect for the advice they share. The problem is that many of them do not know God. A diet of business advice and guidance fed primarily by non-Christian thinkers will condition a person to believe that God is not relevant or "weighty" when it comes to his or her professional endeavors. As Larry Burkett said in his classic book, *Business by the Book*, "The difficulty isn't the advice they give; it's the advice they don't give, specifically, the lack of spiritual insight."[1]

The Holy Spirit often teaches us how to use our spiritual gifts through other people. The Bible says, "Where there is no guidance the people fall, but in abundance of counselors there is victory" (Prov. 11:14). Over the past several years, I have benefitted from the business wisdom of Christian thought leaders such as Dave Ramsey, Dan Miller, Michael Hyatt, John Maxwell, and others. I want to learn about business from people who understand the eternal purpose of business.

In your marketplace endeavors, make sure you are giving priority to the voice of counsel from those who share your Christian values and purpose.

7: Partner with other Christians in your industry.

Jesus partnered with several men in the fishing industry to spread His message. He worked with them at sea. He leveraged their marketplace influence. He used their boats for transportation around the Sea of Galilee. The fishing industry was at the core of his strategy for proclaiming the gospel throughout Israel.

When Paul entered Corinth on one of his missionary journeys, he met Aquila and his wife, Priscilla. The Bible says, "Because he was of the same trade, he stayed with them and they were working, for by trade they were tent-makers" (Acts 18:3). Luke tells us that this couple served as teachers for Apollos, one of the most prominent preachers in the early Church. The Holy

Spirit used their shared, profit-making business interests to connect Paul with this power couple for greater ministry impact (see Rom. 16:3-4; 2 Tim. 4:19; 1 Cor. 16:19).

One of my greatest joys as a Christian entrepreneur has been working with fellow marketplace Christians. We encourage each other, challenge each other, pray for each other, refer clients to each other, and more. The Holy Spirit forms these divine partnerships for the advancement of the gospel.

Discipling an entire industry is the job of all Christians working in that particular sphere of influence. It cannot be accomplished by one person standing behind a pulpit. The Body of Christ cannot function with only a few of its parts. Every person and every spiritual gift are essential for discipling industries, which ultimately will result in the discipleship of nations.

Group Discussion: Which of these seven strategies for transforming your industry for the glory of God stands out to you the most?

---

[1] Larry Burkett, *Business by the Book* (Nashville: Thomas Nelson, 1998), 89.

PART 2

THE MARKETPLACE CHRISTIAN'S TOOLS FOR MINISTRY

*As each has received a gift, use it to serve one another,
as good stewards of God's varied grace.*

—1 PETER 4:10

7

SPIRITUAL GIFTS IN THE MARKETPLACE

SO FAR, WE HAVE CLARIFIED that our primary purpose as marketplace Christians is to spread the awareness of God's glory in our spheres of influence within the marketplace. Now, let's explore the tools God has given to His people for fulfilling this purpose of marketplace ministry.

Examples of Spiritual Gifts in the Marketplace

Marketplace ministry is expressed differently by every marketplace Christian because we all have different combinations of spiritual gifts and because those gifts operate in different settings (i.e. different industries, different cultures, etc.).

For a Christian with the spiritual gift of wisdom, marketplace ministry may mean "applying the wisdom of God to specific business situations." After all, God has given to us the Holy Spirit to lead us "into all truth" (John 16:13), and He has given to us his Word, which is full of timeless business wisdom.

A marketplace Christian with the spiritual gifts of miracle-working and healing might say that marketplace ministry is about "pursuing supernatural signs and wonders in a business setting." Andy Mason leads an organization named Heaven in Business, which trains marketplace Christians in the area of these gifts.

For a Christian with the spiritual gift of intercession, marketplace ministry likely would mean "interceding before God on behalf of my company, co-workers, clients, etc." Amy Everette uses this gift in the marketplace as she leads an organization named Marketplace ROCK, a consulting service that prays for business executives and their companies while teaching these executives how to intercede on behalf of their companies.

A marketplace Christian with the spiritual gift of cross-cultural ministry likely would view marketplace ministry as a calling "to reach foreign lands with the gospel." Ken Eldred emphasizes this aspect of marketplace ministry as he finances and builds multi-million-dollar "kingdom businesses" in India and China to transform these nations with the gospel.

So far, I have mentioned only a few of the spiritual gifts that God has distributed among the hundreds of millions of Christians working in the marketplace. These gifts are to be used by God's people primarily in a business setting. Why? Because that is where 85 percent of the Christian workforce spends the majority of our waking hours. Considering this massive potential for impact, can you imagine what would happen if every Christian in the marketplace was aware of his or her spiritual gifts and started using them in the workplace daily to spread the awareness of God's glory?

How Spiritual Gifts Transcend Natural Abilities in the Marketplace

I often am asked, "What is the difference between a *natural ability* and a *spiritual gift?*" Are Christians supposed to be doing business in the marketplace with natural abilities or with spiritual gifts? Should it be a combination? Should it be mostly one or the other? Is there even a distinction between natural abilities and spiritual gifts?

Most of us would agree that a non-Christian cannot operate with the "gifts of miracle-working and healing," spiritual gifts that Paul mentions in 1 Corinthians 12. In other words, we know that a non-Christian cannot perform a miracle in the name of Jesus.

At the same time, few of us would say that a non-Christian cannot operate with the "gift of administration" or the "gift of leadership," which also are listed as spiritual gifts in the Bible. Many of the *Fortune 500* companies are run by non-Christians that possess extraordinary administrative and leadership abilities. Many of the "*Forbes* 400 Richest People in the World" became wealthy through applying their outstanding administrative and leadership abilities in the marketplace.

As we explore how spiritual gifts transcend natural abilities, let's start with a working definition of a *spiritual gift*:

A spiritual gift is a special ability given by the Holy Spirit through a born-again Christian to the people of God for the purpose of spreading the awareness of the glory of God throughout the earth.

Now, here are six differences between natural abilities and spiritual gifts that will help us to gain a better understanding of spiritual gifts and how we should be using them for marketplace ministry.

Difference 1: Spiritual gifts are only for born-again Christians.

To be sure, natural abilities are equally as God-given as spiritual gifts. Whether we serve God or not, He is the Creator of all people and all of the natural abilities we possess—even the ability to breathe. For Christians and non-Christians alike, we have nothing except that which God has given to us.

However, non-Christians cannot possess "spiritual" gifts—the types of gifts discussed in 1 Corinthians 12, Romans 12, and Ephesians 4—until they become born-again followers of Jesus. Until then, they neither are able nor eligible to receive anything from the Holy Spirit. In fact, people who are not born again cannot even desire the gifts of the Spirit. The Bible says, "The natural person does not accept the things of the Spirit of God, for they are folly to him, and he is not able to understand them because they are spiritually discerned" (1 Cor. 2:14). Unbelievers are content to rely on their natural abilities in their marketplace endeavors.

Difference 2: Spiritual gifts are gifts to the Church through individuals.

When a business professional becomes born-again, his or her natural abilities become spiritual gifts for fulfilling the mission of the Church in the marketplace. These natural abilities become Spirit-empowered spiritual gifts. He or she may also receive gifts that are altogether new such as abilities to work the miracles of God or to speak the revealed Word of God. The gift of administration is just as *spiritual* as the gift of prophecy. Both are necessary for spreading the awareness of the glory of God in the marketplace.

Your spiritual gifts have not been given merely for the purpose of making you and your organization more effective in business. (Yes, that's part of it.) The spiritual gifts you possess as a born-again Christian are, first and foremost, gifts for the Church, the People of God. Not only have they been given for taking care of people within the Church, they have been given for fulfilling the *mission* of the Church. This does not mean your spiritual gifts should be used only when you go to your local church on Sunday. Spiritual gifts are not only for serving Christians. They are for fulfilling the mission of the Church, which is to make disciples of all nations. This point should be fairly obvious, considering one of the spiritual gifts is the "gift of evangelism," a gift that, by definition, must operate among non-believers.

Over the past few decades, spiritual gifts assessments have become excellent tools for local church leaders to mobilize and assign volunteers to serve in their various church programs. Those who score high in the "spiritual gift of hospitality" often are appointed as greeters at the front door of the church on Sunday morning. Those who score high in the gift of "service" often are asked to help with event setup and cleanup around the church building. Certainly, we should offer our spiritual gifts in a way that helps our local churches have outstanding services and excellent programs. This is an essential part of transforming our communities.

Though, *in addition to* using our spiritual gifts to help our local churches, as marketplace Christians, we are called to use our spiritual gifts primarily to fulfill the mission of the Church in the marketplace, partially because that is where most of us spend the majority of our waking hours.

Difference 3: Spiritual gifts are fueled by the fruit of the Spirit.

Natural abilities can be motivated by all sorts of selfish motives. They can help a person to achieve extraordinary worldly and temporary success, gaining massive amounts of money and influence.

Spiritual gifts, on the other hand, can only be fueled by the fruit of the Holy Spirit: "the fruit of the Spirit is love, joy, peace, patience, kindness, goodness, faithfulness, gentleness, self-control" (Gal. 5:22-23). Paul wrote,

> If I have the gift of prophecy, and know all mysteries and all knowledge; and if I have all faith, so as to remove mountains, but do not have love, I am nothing. (1 Cor. 13:2)

Our spiritual gifts are useless for making disciples and changing our industries for the glory of God unless they are motivated by love for the people we are serving. Love and the other fruits of the Spirit provide the passion and proper motivation that fuel our spiritual gifts, enabling us to make an eternal impact in the marketplace.

Unlike spiritual gifts, which are *given* by the Holy Spirit, spiritual fruit must be *cultivated* in partnership with the Holy Spirit. This "fruit" is the Christian character that each of us must develop over time. These fruits are the Christian business ethics and values that we should all be bringing to the marketplace each day. Without this fruit, our spiritual gifts can accomplish nothing for the glory of God in the marketplace.

Difference 4: Spiritual gifts are governed and directed by the Holy Spirit.

A little boy was carrying a heavy rock across the lawn, and his father said, "Son, why don't you put forth all your strength?"

Exhausted, the little boy said, "But, Dad, I am."

And the father replied, "But you haven't asked me to help you."

You can use a natural ability without choosing to rely on the Holy Spirit, but you cannot use a spiritual gift without choosing to rely on the Holy Spirit.

As I mentioned previously, when I first started out as an entrepreneur, I hired a web developer without first praying about whether he was the right one for the job. To make a long story short, I ended up losing $5,000 on account of this person and had nothing to show for it. Choosing to exercise my spiritual gift of wisdom by asking God first could have prevented the loss of six months, $5,000, and my peace of mind during that frustrating season of my life.

As marketplace Christians, we have access to the Holy Spirit's supernatural power in business. This power is demonstrated through our spiritual gifts. Using our spiritual gifts to make disciples of individuals, industries, and nations will come to pass "not by might, nor by power, but by my spirit says the Lord of Hosts" (Zech. 4:6). We can do nothing apart from the Spirit of God, but with God, we can do everything He has created us to do. Jesus said, "Apart from Me, you can do nothing" (John 15:5). This is a humbling, yet liberating truth. Paul wrote, "Not that we are adequate in ourselves to consider anything as coming from ourselves, but our adequacy is from God" (2 Cor. 3:5). When we choose to operate with our spiritual gifts in business, we are choosing to be completely dependent on the power of the Holy Spirit.

The Holy Spirit gives us the confidence to experiment with our gifts in ways that far exceed our natural abilities. As we cultivate an awareness of His presence, we tap into His supernatural power. A believer's awareness of God's presence releases His authority. Our spiritual authority isn't based on how smart we are, how good-looking we are, or how much influence we have with people. When Peter and John demonstrated the supernatural power of God before the Pharisees, the Bible says, "They observed the confidence of Peter and John and understood that they were uneducated and untrained men; they were amazed, and began to recognize them as having been with Jesus" (Acts 4:13). Nothing is more valuable and empowering than the time we invest into getting to know God and getting filled with His matchless strength. Without His power, we can do nothing of eternal value. However, with His power, we can do all things through Christ who strengthens us (Phil. 4:13).

Difference 5: Spiritual gifts enable us to worship God through our work.

Sir Christopher Wren, the prominent English architect, was supervising the construction of a magnificent cathedral in London. As the legend goes, a local journalist thought it would be interesting to interview some of the workers, so he asked three of them the following question: "What do you do here?"

The first replied, "I'm cutting stone for merely 10 shillings a day, but at least it pays my bills."

The next answered, "I'm putting in 10 long hours every day on this mindless job."

But the third worker proudly declared, "I'm helping Sir Christopher Wren construct one of London's greatest cathedrals!"

"Excellence," said Booker T. Washington, "is to do a common thing in an uncommon way." God is worthy of our best; therefore, He despises and rejects mediocre, half-hearted effort. He expects us to fulfill every assignment wholeheartedly and at the apex of our God-given ability. The Bible says, "Whatever your hand finds to do, do it with all your might" (Ecc. 9:10).

If your work is performed wholeheartedly and for the purpose of spreading the awareness of God's glory, Jesus Christ, it has been performed with spiritual gifts and is considered an offering of worship to God. In its different forms, the word, "work," appears more than 800 times in the Bible. That's more than all the words used to express worship, music, praise, and singing combined! Regardless of your current assignment along your vocational path, "Whatever you do, do it with all your heart as unto the Lord, not working for men. It is the Lord Christ whom you serve" (Col. 3:23). Don't go to work just for monetary benefits. Go to work for Jesus by allowing the Holy Spirit to work through your spiritual gifts in the marketplace.

Difference 6: Spiritual gifts can produce eternal results and rewards.

Before we became born-again Christians, we could not use our natural abilities to produce eternal results and rewards. Yes, God can use anyone for his purposes, even people who have not voluntarily yielded their lives to him. In the Old Testament, He even spoke through a donkey (Num. 21:22-39). However, only spiritual gifts fueled by the fruit of the Holy Spirit for the work of the Holy Spirit can produce eternal results and rewards.

The bottom line for marketplace ministers is not merely financial, social, environmental, or anything else that is temporary. The bottom line for marketplace ministers is eternal. Spiritual gifts enable us to do the work of the Holy Spirit, the fruit of which is the only return on investment that will last in eternity. This eternally valuable work is to make disciples of all nations, spreading the awareness of God's glory. If it doesn't last in eternity, it's not the bottom line. The Bible says,

> ...each man's work will become evident; for the day will show it because it is to be revealed with fire, and the fire itself will test the quality of each man's work. If any man's work which he has built on it remains, he will receive a reward. If any man's work is burned up, he will suffer loss; but he himself will be saved, yet so as through fire.
> (1 Cor. 3:13-15)

Your spiritual gifts are God's business.

In the *Book of Genesis*, Pharaoh had a dream about an impending famine that would have devastated the entire Egyptian Empire if no one had been able to interpret his dream (Gen. 41:14-37). Because Joseph had a strong reputation as one who was able to interpret dreams, he was summoned to reveal the meaning of Pharaoh's perplexing dream. When he was asked for the interpretation, Joseph responded, "Interpreting dreams is God's business" (Gen. 40:8b). He was dependent on the Holy Spirit's power to accomplish the task, and he knew that this spiritual power would only be made available to those who would use it to spread the awareness of God's glory.

When you are faced with challenges in the marketplace, choose to derive your ability from the Holy Spirit. Just as Joseph responded to his challenge by saying, "Interpreting dreams is God's business," the same should be said about each of the spiritual gifts. For example,

- "**Administration** is God's business."
- "**Prophecy** is God's business."
- "**Leadership** is God's business."
- "**Wisdom** is God's business."
- "**Encouragement** is God's business."

Once you have identified your own primary spiritual gifts, fill in the blank:

"(*My spiritual gift*) is God's business."

Acknowledge that God is the Source of every ability you need in the marketplace. Refuse to rely on the feebleness of human strength. As long as you are committed to spreading the awareness of His glory and not your own counterfeit glory, God can make you more effective than you ever thought possible.

The marketplace is desperate for your spiritual gifts.

Your spiritual gifts are in demand in the marketplace. The Bible says, "A man's gift makes room for him and brings him before great men" (Prov. 18:16). The results promised in Proverbs 18:16 only happen when the gift has been given away in worship to God and in service to others.

For example, those in need of guidance in business need Christians with the gifts of knowledge, discernment, wisdom, prophecy, and leadership.

Those who lack creativity need Christians with the gift of creativity.

Those hungry to learn need Christians who have the gift of teaching.

After warning Pharaoh about the encroaching national crisis depicted in the dream, "Pharaoh said to Joseph, 'See, I have set you over all the land of Egypt'" (Gen. 41:41). His gift to interpret dreams led to the Holy Spirit using his gift of administration to manage a feeding program for the entire empire. His gifts made a place for him as he used them to spread the awareness of God's glory. His gift placed him before a man with great influence, and Joseph had a pure heart that enabled him to use it for the glory of God.

Discover what God has made you good at, surrender that gift into His service, and watch Him open doors for you to spread the awareness of Jesus in your industry and beyond. Our spiritual gifts have been given by God to help the people we influence in the marketplace to become more like Jesus Christ. That includes our customers, clients, vendors, co-workers, bosses, board members, shareholders, social media followers, and anyone else that comes in contact with us in the marketplace. The degree to which we are fulfilling this mandate is the true "bottom line" for every Christian in business.

Group Discussion: In what ways are you uniquely gifted to do your part in the disciple-making mission of the Church? Here's another way to ask this question: What are your spiritual gifts? Leadership? Administration? Prophecy? Creativity? Wisdom? There are many more.

8

RECEIVING YOUR SPIRITUAL GIFTS

WHEN I ASK Bible-believing business professionals to name a passage of the Bible that relates to doing business, they often first mention Jesus' "Parable of the Talents" (Matt. 25:14-30). I believe this is because this parable offers a perspective of God that we usually don't hear about in church. In this parable, God isn't being presented as Father, Son, Holy Spirit, Savior, Friend, Creator, or Miracle-Worker. In this parable, God is presented as a businessman. Because we spend a significant portion of our lives in a business setting as marketplace Christians, viewing God as a businessman comes quite naturally for many of us.

Here are a few lessons about using our spiritual gifts in marketplace ministry that we can learn from the "Parable of the Talents."

God invests spiritual gifts in His people.

Although the master in the parable did not give each of the three stewards equal amounts of currency, they each received at least one talent to invest. A single talent was equivalent to the standard pay for approximately 20 years of labor (about $500,000 USD), a significant amount of money.

Likewise, God has given a measure of spiritual gifts to every Christian, but He has not given the same spiritual gifts to every person. Through the Holy Spirit, God has distributed these gifts "just as he wills" (1 Cor. 12:11). Paul writes that "we have gifts that differ according to the grace given to us" (Rom. 12:6). While some people have the same spiritual gifts, we have them in different measures, and they will be expressed differently. They are to be thought of as "grace gifts" and not as "personal strengths" because they are expressions of God and not of ourselves.

God assigns purposes for His spiritual gifts.

In the "Parable of the Talents," the master gave a clear, implicit assignment to his stewards: "bring back more money than I'm giving to you." He expected and demanded returns on his investments in his stewards.

No matter the gift or the measure of the gift, God expects an eternal return on his investments. He expects us to use His gifts for the purposes for which He assigned them. For marketplace Christians, this purpose is to spread the awareness of the glory of God throughout our spheres of influence.

God rewards our diligence and productivity.

The stewards in the "Parable of the Talents" worked in an economic system in which they could be rewarded in proportion to their efforts and productivity. The parable affirms that God rewards hard work, an ethic that any successful business professional can appreciate. When the master returned from his journey, he said to one of the two diligent stewards, "Well done, good and faithful slave. You were faithful with a few things, I will put you in charge of many things; enter into the joy of your master" (Matt. 25:23). Faithful stewardship over what they had been entrusted resulted in even more responsibilities for the two faithful stewards.

In the parable, the diligence and productivity of the two faithful stewards is contrasted with the slothfulness of the "wicked, lazy slave" (Matt. 25:26). Not only does God reward diligence, he punishes laziness. This is how the marketplace works.

The Bible teaches us that we "should earnestly desire the most helpful gifts" (1 Cor. 12:31). But God will not give additional responsibilities and gifts until we are faithful, diligent, and productive with the spiritual gifts and marketplace ministry assignments we have right now.

God trusts us to use His gifts.

In the parable, before the master went away on his journey, he told three of his stewards, "I'm leaving, and I'm placing you three in charge." The master would not have entrusted his possessions to the stewards if he did not trust them. The parable shows us that God has entrusted a certain amount of decision-making autonomy to his people. He trusts us because He loves us, and "love always trusts" (1 Cor. 13:7). In addition to spiritual gifts, consider what God has entrusted to His people:

- Everything pertaining to life and godliness (2 Pet. 1:3)
- Every spiritual blessing in heavenly places (Eph. 1:3)
- His mission (Matt. 28:16-20)
- His Word (John 17:14)
- The earth (Gen. 1:28)

- His glory (John 17:22)
- The keys to the kingdom of heaven (Matt. 16:19)
- His mysteries (1 Cor. 4:1)
- The power to produce wealth (Deut. 8:18)
- A great name (Gen. 12:2)
- The temple of God (1 Cor. 6:18-19)
- Callings (Rom. 11:29)
- His only Son (John 3:16)
- Everything we have (1 Cor. 4:7)

God wants us to see the world the way He sees it.

When the master returned, notice he didn't say to the faithful stewards, "Now, give me my money, and get back to work!" Instead, he invited them to "enter into the joy of your master" (Matt. 25:23, NASB). In other words, he wanted them to recognize that they were in partnership together. He didn't view them merely as tools to get things done. The master wanted his stewards to see things from his own perspective.

God wants us to see the marketplace as He sees it. He wants us to see our co-workers and customers the way He sees them. He wants us to see the marketplace not as a hopeless place or as a place only for exercising selfish ambition. God has entrusted spiritual gifts to us because wants us to partner with Him in spreading the awareness of Jesus so the world will accept and represent His Son.

Group Discussion: What business lesson from the "Parable of the Talents" stands out to you the most? How does the "Parable of the Talents" relate to using your spiritual gifts in the marketplace?

PART 3

SPIRITUAL GIFTS IN THE MARKETPLACE ASSESSMENT

INSTRUCTIONS

- For each of the spiritual gift recognition statements, please rate yourself on a scale of 1-10 in the corresponding blanks on the Response Sheet provided on page #87. (1 = "Never", 10 = "Always and without exception")
- You can download a blank copy of the Response Sheet at the following link: www.TheologyofBusiness.com/ResponseSheet
- For the most helpful results on this assessment:
  - Spend no more than 20 seconds on each item. Go with your first instinct. Your immediate response is best.
  - Remember that the goal is not to score high for any of the spiritual gift recognition statements. The goal is to have variances among your responses so that you can identify your primary spiritual gifts.
  - Be as honest with your answers as possible. This will produce the most helpful results.

Spiritual Gift Recognition Statements

1. "I organize ideas, resources, time, and people effectively."
2. "Ministry leaders look to me for guidance."
3. "People tell me I am a compassionate person."
4. "I like introducing people to each other."
5. "I enjoy creating and/or inventing new things and new ways of doing things."
6. "I am passionate about connecting with people from other cultures and nationalities."
7. "I have a unique ability to sense whether or not a person is acting in accordance with God's will."
8. "Through inspirational words, I often have helped people to think more optimistically about themselves and the world around them."
9. "I have challenged other Christians to share their faith with non-Christians."
10. "I have found it somewhat easy to believe God for things that seemed impossible to others."
11. "I regularly give money beyond my tithe toward the Lord's work."
12. "People often tell me I made them feel welcome in a new place."
13. "I am passionate about praying to God on behalf of others."
14. "I spend a significant percentage of my time learning new things."
15. "People often tell me I am a gifted leader."
16. "I am passionate about pursuing opportunities to see God work miracles wherever I go."

17. "I often take the time to care for the emotional and/or spiritual needs of people around me."
18. "I have communicated to others timely and urgent messages that I believe came directly from God."
19. "People around me know they can count on me to help out."
20. "I am passionate about putting in the extra effort to explain complicated concepts in a simple way so that people can understand."
21. "I often speak to God in an unknown, heavenly language."
22. "I apply the truth of God's Word in my everyday life."
23. "Others have told me I helped to lead them into the presence of God."
24. "People have told me I am a good planner and organizer."
25. "I have started multiple new ministries."
26. "My heart hurts when I see others hurting."
27. "I have connected many like-minded people together."
28. "People have told me I am a very creative person."
29. "I gravitate toward people who are from different cultures and nationalities than mine."
30. "Others have told me I have a special ability to perceive things most people are not able to perceive."
31. "I am passionate about motivating people to be more courageous."
32. "I am passionate about sharing the gospel message with all types of people."
33. "People tell me I have a large amount of faith."
34. "Giving is one of my favorite things to do."
35. "I have invited guests into my home on a regular basis."
36. "People ask me to pray for them because they know I actually will pray."
37. "My life demonstrates that I am passionate about learning new things."

38. "I prefer to focus on the bigger picture while other people work on the details."
39. "When people need a miracle to happen in their lives, such as a healing miracle, they often ask me to pray for them."
40. "I am passionate about connecting with, caring for, and coaching others one-on-one."
41. "I don't mind confronting people about their faulty thinking."
42. "I enjoy doing the tasks my leaders don't have time to do."
43. "I teach everywhere I go… not just in a classroom setting."
44. "To strengthen myself spiritually, I speak to my spirit regularly in an unknown, heavenly language."
45. "I intuitively find solutions to complicated problems."
46. "Throughout the day, I am keenly aware of the presence, majesty, and goodness of God."
47. "I enjoy figuring out what needs to get done to accomplish larger objectives."
48. "God tends to place me before influential people to represent him and His Kingdom."
49. "I am passionate about helping to alleviate people's sufferings."
50. "People have told me I am good at networking."
51. "I have created many new things and/or new ways of doing things."
52. "People have told me I should be a missionary in another culture."
53. "I believe I have a special responsibility to sense when situations are spiritually unhealthy."
54. "People have told me they feel encouraged when they are around me."
55. "I have led many people to Jesus during my lifetime."
56. "I am passionate about trusting God to do big things."

57. "People who know me well would say I am a generous person."
58. "I am passionate about helping strangers to feel welcome when they are in my presence."
59. "I pray for extended amounts of time concerning the needs in our world."
60. "People view me as a source of information."
61. "I am passionate about getting other people involved and leveraging their unique abilities to accomplish large objectives."
62. "I have prayed for specific miracles, signs, wonders, and healings to happen and have seen many of them come to pass."
63. "People often share their personal struggles with me because they trust me."
64. "Other people have confirmed that they believe I speak God's truth about specific situations."
65. "I am eager to help even when others are not."
66. "People have told me I am a good teacher."
67. "I have spoken a message from God to others in an unknown, heavenly language that I or someone else interpreted."
68. "People often ask me how to deal with confusing situations."
69. "I set apart time every day to worship God and invite his presence into my life and into the atmosphere around me wherever I go."

RESPONSE SHEET

A blank PDF copy of this response sheet can be downloaded at www.TheologyofBusiness.com/ResponseSheet.

TOTALS

1. ____	24. ____	47. ____	A. _____
2. ____	25. ____	48. ____	B. _____
3. ____	26. ____	49. ____	C. _____
4. ____	27. ____	50. ____	D. _____
5. ____	28. ____	51. ____	E. _____
6. ____	29. ____	52. ____	F. _____
7. ____	30. ____	53. ____	G. _____
8. ____	31. ____	54. ____	H. _____
9. ____	32. ____	55. ____	I. _____
10. ____	33. ____	56. ____	J. _____
11. ____	34. ____	57. ____	K. _____
12. ____	35. ____	58. ____	L. _____
13. ____	36. ____	59. ____	M. _____
14. ____	37. ____	60. ____	N. _____
15. ____	38. ____	61. ____	O. _____
16. ____	39. ____	62. ____	P. _____
17. ____	40. ____	63. ____	Q. _____
18. ____	41. ____	64. ____	R. _____
19. ____	42. ____	65. ____	S. _____
20. ____	43. ____	66. ____	T. _____
21. ____	44. ____	67. ____	U. _____
22.	45.	68.	V.
23. ____	46. ____	69. ____	W. _____

CALCULATING THE RESULTS

For each line on the Response Sheet, add the three numbers across for each letter, and write the totals next to each corresponding letter. (For example, your responses for #1 plus #24 plus #47 would add up to the amount you would place in the blank for "A," which is the gift of administration.) Then, write-in the corresponding spiritual gifts and circle your top three or four highest-scoring spiritual gifts.

A = Administration
B = Apostleship
C = Compassion
D = Connecting
E = Creativity
F = Cross-Cultural Ministry
G = Discernment
H = Encouragement
I = Evangelism
J = Faith
K = Giving
L = Hospitality
M = Intercessory Prayer

N = Knowledge
O = Leadership
P = Miracle-Working &
        Healing
Q = Pastoring
R = Prophecy
S = Service
T = Teaching
U = Tongues &
        Interpretation
V = Wisdom
W = Worship

PART 4

SPIRITUAL GIFTS IN THE MARKETPLACE PROFILES

A "spiritual gift" is a special ability given by the Holy Spirit through a born-again Christian to the people of God for the purpose of spreading the awareness of the glory of God throughout the earth.

Administration

The gift of administration is the special ability to spread the awareness of God's glory by organizing resources and people to accomplish specific goals.

Where the gift of administration is lacking, there is frustration, overwhelm, chaos, and ineffectiveness in the workplace. If you have the gift of administration, you can create order out of chaos, resulting in a sense of peace for your customers, coworkers, supervisors, and everyone else in your sphere of influence in the marketplace. You bring a sense of stability and comfort to those you serve in business. Most organizations would be utterly ineffective without having people like you on their teams to implement the plans and achieve the goals of the organization.

Gift Recognition Statements

- "I have organized ideas, resources, time, and people effectively."
- "I enjoy figuring out what needs to get done to accomplish larger objectives."
- "People have told me I am a good planner and organizer."

Marketplace Impact

Michael Hyatt, the former CEO and Chairman of Thomas Nelson Publishers, uses his spiritual gift of administration to help people achieve more in their personal and professional lives through effectiveness, efficiency, and maintaining the right priorities. One of his readers described why he needs what Michael has to offer by saying,

> I feel overwhelmed. No matter what I'm doing, I feel like I should be doing something else. When I'm traveling for work, I am missing my daughter's soccer game. When I make the game, I can hardly resist the impulse to pull my phone out of my pocket and check my email. I constantly wonder if I'm missing something important at work.[1]

Using his gift of administration, Michael ministers to these types of people by helping them to identify what is most important and then formulating a plan of action to help them achieve their desired results. Michael said, "If you're like me, that means making your relationship with God, your health, your marriage, relationships with your friends, your church, and your contribution to your community top priorities."[2] He helps people to create order out of chaos in their personal and professional lives.

Although his speaking and writing revolves around the theme of "Intentional Leadership," his blog originally began with a sharp focus on the theme of productivity. His focus on effectiveness and efficiency is a hallmark of the gift of administration. Michael has a tremendous ability to help people get more of the right things done in their personal and professional lives.

When Michael Hyatt speaks, people listen. As of the time of this writing, his blog has more than 540,000 subscribers. As expressions of his gift of administration, Michael shares administrative advice such as "How to Shave 10 Hours off Your Workweek," "How to Create a Life Plan," and "How Evernote Can Make You a Better, Faster Blogger."

Biblical Insights

- Genesis 1:2
- Luke 14:28-30
- Acts 6:1-7
- 1 Corinthians 12:28
- Titus 1:4-5

Do you have an example of a marketplace Christian who uses the gift of administration in a business setting? To encourage other marketplace Christians who have this gift, please share your example by commenting at the following link where you also will find additional resources and information about how this gift can be used for the glory of God in the marketplace:

www.TheologyofBusiness.com/GiftOfAdministration

---

[1] http://michaelhyatt.com/start-here

[2] Ibid.

APOSTLESHIP

The gift of apostleship is the special ability to spread the awareness of God's glory by starting new ministries and demonstrating spiritual authority in a particular sphere of influence.

Those with the gift of apostleship in the marketplace are usually the first to recognize the need to organize, train, and equip Christians for ministry in the marketplace. Upon the prompting of the Holy Spirit, they are the ones who initiate marketplace ministry movements within their own spheres of influence. They are the ones to whom other ministry leaders look for leadership in new and unfamiliar ministry environments.

The marketplace ministry of those with the gift of apostleship usually is characterized by the theme of "spiritual authority." They often aim to be like Joseph, Daniel, Esther, and other biblical heroes God promoted to high levels of influence in the world's institutions.

Gift Recognition Statements

- "I have started multiple new ministries."
- "Ministry leaders look to me for guidance."
- "God tends to place me before influential people to represent him and his Kingdom."

Marketplace Impact

Lance Wallnau, founder of LanceLearning.org, has the gift of apostleship. He mobilizes Christians to exercise their God-given authority to transform the culture around them. He teaches

Christians to walk in the dominion of Jesus and ascend the "Mountain of Business" for the glory of God, one of the "Seven Mountains" of cultural influence. Lance believes that "unprecedented economic, political, and social shaking will create extraordinary opportunities for leaders willing to climb to the top of their mountain, leverage the platform God has given them, and advance kingdom interests."[1] He helps people to "find clarity in their assignment, develop mastery in their field, step into convergence, and function within their passion."[2] This is the language and behavior of those with the gift of apostleship.

Biblical Insights

- Acts 15:22-35
- 1 Corinthians 12:28
- 2 Corinthians 12:12
- Galatians 2:7-10
- Ephesians 4:11-14

Do you have an example of a marketplace Christian who uses the gift of apostleship in a business setting? To encourage other marketplace Christians who have this gift, please share your example by commenting at the following link where you also will find additional resources and information about how this gift can be used for the glory of God in the marketplace:

www.TheologyofBusiness.com/GiftOfApostleship

---

[1] http://lancewallnau.com/about/
[2] Ibid.

COMPASSION

The gift of compassion is the special ability to spread the awareness of God's glory by feeling genuine empathy and compassion for individuals who are hurting.

Marketplace ministers with the gift of compassion help business professionals never to forget that people are not merely consumers, employees, prospects, investors, subscribers, etc. First and foremost, people are people, so they should not be treated merely like numbers, objects, or cogs to get things done in the marketplace. Each person has a story that needs to be heard and needs that need to be met.

Gift Recognition Statements

- "I am passionate about helping to alleviate people's sufferings."
- "My heart hurts when I see others hurting."
- "People tell me I am a compassionate person."

Marketplace Impact

As the owner and CEO of a manufacturing company named Polydeck, Peter Freissle setup a "Caring Committee" for his employees. This Caring Committee is responsible for implementing and managing numerous care and compassion programs to meet emergency financial needs for the employees in his company. These programs included an employee home repair fund, employee emergency loan fund, employee car repair fund, and a medical emergency fund to meet specific needs among the company's staff members and their families.

Jerry, one of the Polydeck employees who received compassionate assistance from the company during his time of dire need said,

> The company surrounded me at a time of difficulty, helping me with my daughter that has osteoscaroma, which is bone cancer. The Caring Committee presented an envelope to all the employees in the plant, and everybody pitched in, and it came out to be almost two thousand dollars.[1]

Biblical Insights

- Matthew 9:35-36
- Mark 9:41
- Luke 10:29-37
- Romans 12:8
- 1 Thessalonians 5:14

Do you have an example of a marketplace Christian who uses the gift of compassion in a business setting? To encourage other marketplace Christians who have this gift, please share your example by commenting at the following link where you also will find additional resources and information about how this gift can be used for the glory of God in the marketplace:

www.TheologyofBusiness.com/GiftOfCompassion.

---

[1] Dr. Steve O. Steff, *The Business Card* (USA: Lanphier Press, 2012), 149.

CONNECTING

The gift of connecting is the special ability to spread the awareness of God's glory by facilitating interactions between like-minded individuals.

Those with the gift of connecting are great networkers. People with this gift are great at matching the right people with the right people and opportunities for the benefit of the Kingdom of God.

Gift Recognition Statements

- "I have connected many like-minded people together."
- "I like introducing people to each other."
- "People have told me I am good at networking."

Marketplace Impact

Pure Flix Entertainment is the largest Christian film production and distribution company in the world. It has produced films such as *Do You Believe?*, *Woodlawn*, and *God's Not Dead*, which has earned more than $62 million.

In 2009, the founder of Pure Flix, Russell Wolfe, met Steve Fedyski, who was using his spiritual gift of connecting as the CEO of Pinnacle Forum, an organization dedicated to "building a network of leaders committed to personal and cultural transformation centered on the values of Jesus."[1] When they met, Russell was struggling to grow his company, but Steve resonated with Russell's passion to transform the culture for Christ through entertainment.

From that time forward, Steve began to use his spiritual gift of connecting and his influence with Pinnacle Forum to help Russell fulfill his God-given dream to produce and distribute great Christian films. At nearly all of Steve's 100 speaking engagements each year following their initial meeting, Steve shared Russell's dream with the audience. At each event, he gathered the contact information of anyone who was interested in helping to promote Russell's films. This contact information was used to pack out film screenings with key influencers at key locations all over the United States.

As a result of Steve's efforts to connect Russell with people who could help him, approximately 80 percent of the current investors in Pure Flix Entertainment are members of Pinnacle Forum, the network led by Steve.

In 2015, Steve was named the Chief Operations Officer of Pure Flix Entertainment and continues to play a lead role in the success of the company.

Biblical Insights

- John 1:45; 4:39-42

Do you have an example of a marketplace Christian who uses the gift of connecting in a business setting? To encourage other marketplace Christians who have this gift, please share your example by commenting at the following link where you also will find additional resources and information about how this gift can be used for the glory of God in the marketplace:

www.TheologyofBusiness.com/GiftOfConnecting

---

[1] http://pinnacleforum.com/about/#our-mission

CREATIVITY

The gift of creativity is the special ability to spread the awareness of God's glory by creating things and/or new ways of doing things.

Marketplace Christians with the spiritual gift of creativity reveal the creative power and genius of God in the business world. In the marketplace, people with this gift often are referred to as "innovators" and "disruptors" of the status quo in their respective industries.

Gift Recognition Statements

- "I have created many new things and/or new ways of doing things."
- "I enjoy creating and/or inventing new things and new ways of doing things."
- "People have told me that I am a very creative person."

Marketplace Impact

Sensing the call to become "God's businessman," R.G. LeTourneau decided to use his God-given gift of creativity in the marketplace. He was awarded 299 patents for his earth-moving and materials handling equipment. These inventions included bulldozers, scrapers, portable cranes, rollers, dump wagons, bridge spans, logging equipment, mobile sea platforms for oil exploration, the electric wheel, and many others. Approximately 70 percent of the earth-moving equipment used by the Allies to win World War II was manufactured by his company.

LaTourneau was committed to using his business as a tool for making disciples of Jesus. He hired full-time chaplains to work in his factories, caring for his workers and teaching the Bible to them. He admonished his fellow business owners, "Unless we businessmen… testify that Christianity is the driving power of our business, you'll always have doubters claiming that religion is all talk and no production."[1]

Biblical Insights

- Genesis 1:1
- Exodus 31:1-11
- Acts 18:2-3

Do you have an example of a marketplace Christian who uses the gift of creativity in a business setting? To encourage other marketplace Christians who have this gift, please share your example by commenting at the following link where you also will find additional resources and information about how this gift can be used for the glory of God in the marketplace:

www.TheologyofBusiness.com/GiftOfCreativity

---

[1] *Mover of Men and Mountains: The Autobiography of R.G. LeTourneau* (Chicago: Moody Press, 1967), 203.

Cross-Cultural Ministry

The gift of cross-cultural ministry is the special ability to spread the awareness of God's glory by ministering to people in a significantly different culture.

People who ask to be admitted into foreign countries as "missionaries" are no longer being admitted into many nations around the world. However, these same "closed" nations are eager to allow business professionals to live and work within their borders, regardless of their religious affiliations.

Business professionals with the gift of cross-cultural ministry should consider doing business in other parts of the world, using their businesses as platforms for revealing the glory of God.

Gift Recognition Statements

- "I am passionate about connecting with people from other cultures and nationalities."
- "I gravitate toward people who are from different cultures and nationalities than mine."
- "People have told me I should be a missionary in another culture."

Marketplace Impact

Ken Eldred uses his gift of cross-cultural ministry to finance and build multi-million-dollar "kingdom businesses" in India and China to transform these nations with the gospel. He co-owns a call center in India that was founded to spread the gospel and make disciples throughout the country.

Although the country's population is only five percent Christian, approximately 60 percent of the company's 1500 employees are Christians. Local pastors nominate members of their congregations as prospective employees of the company, many of whom are young and recent college graduates. These young people gain valuable work experience and discipleship training at the call center. Then, they move on to greater positions of influence throughout India and beyond. Ken explained,

> You will know if you have a gift of cross-cultural ministry. The Lord will confirm it with introductions and situations that compel you to make a difference from right where you are, step by step. But, you must submit all your plans to him and ask him to show you your mission. The mission he gave me has been the same for almost 40 years ago. The twists and turns are up to God. The adventure is exciting but unpredictable. Seek ye first the Kingdom of Heaven and all these things will be added unto you.

Biblical Insights

- Acts 8:4, 27; 13:2-3; 22:21
- Romans 10:15

Do you have an example of a marketplace Christian who uses the gift of cross-cultural ministry in a business setting? To encourage other marketplace Christians who have this gift, please share your example by commenting at the following link where you also will find additional resources and information about how this gift can be used for the glory of God in the marketplace:

www.TheologyofBusiness.com/GiftOfCrossCulturalMinistry

Discernment

The gift of discernment is the special ability to spread the awareness of God's glory by perceiving accurately whether certain behavior is divine, human, or satanic.

Those with the gift of discernment can protect their companies from spiritual attacks that might come in the form of bad business partners, bad business deals, and other hazardous business situations that cannot be perceived by the natural mind.

Gift Recognition Statements

- "I believe I have a special responsibility to sense when situations are spiritually unhealthy."
- "I have a unique ability to sense whether or not a person is acting in accordance with God's will."
- "Others have told me I have a special ability to perceive things that most people are not able to perceive."

Marketplace Impact

A Christian business professional named Paul uses his gift of discernment in the information security industry by helping businesses and government agencies solve difficult security challenges.

Over the years, his supernatural effectiveness in profiling people and solving complex problems has caused multiple business leaders and government employees to ask him, "What's your secret?" When Paul was asked this question at the end of a training class he led for an agency of the United States intelligence community, he responded, "I am a servant of the most high God..." In front of a room full of elite government agents, he shared his faith in God.

He then explained to the audience how the Holy Spirit gives various spiritual gifts to those who are sons and daughters of God and have sought the Holy Spirit and His gifts. He shared that one of his primary spiritual gifts is discernment, which helps him to glorify God through upholding justice as an information security expert and practitioner.

After he finished, the entire room erupted in applause due to Paul's boldness in sharing his beliefs. Afterward, individual agents came to him personally to ask more questions about his faith.

Biblical Insights

- Matthew 16:21-23
- Acts 5:1-11; 16:16-18
- 1 Corinthians 12:10
- 1 John 4:1-6

Do you have an example of a marketplace Christian who uses the gift of discernment in a business setting? To encourage other marketplace Christians who have this gift, please share your example by commenting at the following link where you also will find additional resources and information about how this gift can be used for the glory of God in the marketplace:

www.TheologyofBusiness.com/GiftOfDiscernment

ENCOURAGEMENT

The gift of encouragement is the special ability to spread the awareness of God's glory by inspiring others to be more courageous.

Gift Recognition Statements

- "Through inspirational words, I often have helped people to think more optimistically about themselves and the world around them."
- "I am passionate about motivating people to be more courageous."
- "People have told me they feel encouraged when they are around me."

Marketplace Impact

According to Lifetime Television, Mary K. Ash (1918-2001), founder of Mary Kay Cosmetics, was the "Most Outstanding Woman in Business in the 20th Century." She used her spiritual gift of encouragement to help women become all that God created them to be.

Prior to starting Mary Kay Cosmetics, Mary Kay spent 25 years working in a sales position in corporate America. During that time, she repeatedly was refused promotions and pay raises the men were getting. In response to the unjust way in which she and other women were being treated in the marketplace, she decided to start a company that would encourage women to achieve their fullest potential. She said,

> If you ask me, "What is the common denominator among women?"… it is the fact that most of us, most women, don't believe in their own God-given ability. So what we do is try to show them how great they really are.[1]

As of 2014, her company had wholesale volume in excess of $3 billion and approximately three million sales consultants. The company culture she created infused boldness and courage into women worldwide.

She credited the success of her company to its decision to "take God as our partner." She based her founding principle on the Golden Rule: "do unto others as you would have them do unto you" (Luke 6:31). She redefined business terms like "P & L" to mean "people and love." She taught her sales consultants to keep "God first, family second, career third."

Current National Sales Director for Mary Kay, Dorothy Boyd, shared with me about the way Mary Kay encouraged her personally:

> I came to Mary Kay in 1982, so I have grown up in the business. Before Mary Kay, I didn't have the tools to recognize my self-doubt. Mary Kay gave me the courage to step out of receiving a secure paycheck from a traditional job, walk by faith, become a successful entrepreneur, take care of my family, and become the best that I could be.
>
> When you get around women who are positive and encouraging like Mary Kay, it's like being on a different planet, a planet where the possibilities are unlimited. I often heard Mary Kay say, "Most people haven't received a round of applause

since they graduated from high school, so we should encourage our people by praising them onward toward success." Truly, in our company, every little effort in the right direction is acknowledged and recognized. And the large wins are beautifully rewarded! Coming from the thankless experience of teaching art to high school kids for three years, I literally was starved for both praise and recognition (and didn't even know it) when I became immersed in this positive culture in 1982.

Mary Kay also believed that there was no such thing as 'constructive' criticism. She believed that all criticism is destructive, so her mother's words, "You *can* do it!", were passed on to everyone she met. In the very rare event that something negative must be addressed, she taught us to 'sandwich it between two thick, heavy layers of praise.' She truly created a positive environment completely devoid of harsh judgement in which fledgling young entrepreneurs like me could find a safe place to learn, grow, and gain confidence both personally and professionally.

As I look around me within the field sales force of our company, I am continually gratified to know and observe thousands of women whose lives have been enriched by Mary Kay's daily use of her gift of encouragement. Encouragement speaks any language, and our company is now in 35 countries around the world.

Biblical Insights

- Acts 14:22
- Romans 12:8
- 1 Timothy 4:13
- Hebrews 10:24-25

Do you have an example of a marketplace Christian who uses the gift of encouragement in a business setting? To encourage other marketplace Christians who have this gift, please share your example by commenting at the following link where you also will find additional resources and information about how this gift can be used for the glory of God in the marketplace:

www.TheologyofBusiness.com/GiftOfEncouragement

---

1 "Mary Kay's Golden Year Full of History & Vision," *CBNnews.com* (December 31, 2013), http://www.cbn.com/cbnnews/us/2013/December/Mary-Kay-Cosmetics-Golden-Year-Full-of-History--Vision/.

EVANGELISM

The gift of evangelism is the special ability to spread the awareness of God's glory by sharing the gospel message with unbelievers in such a way that men and women become Jesus' disciples and responsible members of the body of Christ.
Marketplace Christians with this gift are passionate about articulating the gospel message for their co-workers, clients, customers, supervisors, vendors, etc.

Gift Recognition Statements

- "I have led many people to Jesus during my lifetime."
- "I am passionate about sharing the gospel message with all types of people."
- "I have challenged other Christians to share their faith with non-Christians."

Marketplace Impact

Evangelism is one of Robert's primary spiritual gifts. For the past 35 years, he has worked as an expert witness for attorneys who defend people who have lost large sums of money entrusted to their stockbrokers. Because of his expertise as a former stockbroker himself, Robert has been called in by these attorneys more than 1500 times to interview their clients, many of whom are senior citizens and widows. Robert's expertise concerning the financial industry helps these attorneys build their cases against stockbrokers and financial institutions they believe have taken advantage of their clients.

As you can imagine, the people Robert interviews usually are in extremely desperate situations and are in search of hope and vindication. Over the course of the entire year leading up to each trial, Robert has pointed these people toward Jesus, the One who offers true salvation. Robert reported that, in nearly each of the 1500 times he has met with a client, he has prayed for the person to receive Jesus as his or her personal Savior—unless the person was already a Christian. Almost every non-Christian person he has prayed for in these office settings has become a Christian. If the person was already a believer, he would pray that he or she would experience even greater joy and power through the Holy Spirit.

Not only would he pray with the clients to receive Jesus, he would pray with the attorneys to receive Jesus. One of the attorneys he led to the Lord went from being a depressed alcoholic to becoming a joyful, Christ-centered philanthropist who went on to start one of the largest law firms of its kind in the United States. He and Robert are close friends and brothers-in-Christ to this day.

Biblical Insights

- Acts 8:5-6, 26-40; 14:21; 21:8
- Ephesians 4:11-14

Do you have an example of a marketplace Christian who uses the gift of evangelism in a business setting? To encourage other marketplace Christians who have this gift, please share your example by commenting at the following link where you also will find additional resources and information about how this gift can be used for the glory of God in the marketplace:

www.TheologyofBusiness.com/GiftOfEvangelism

FAITH

The gift of faith is the special ability to spread the awareness of God's glory by believing that God will do things that are impossible for humans to do apart from His intervention.

Gift Recognition Statements

- "I am passionate about trusting God to do big things."
- "I have found it somewhat easy to believe God for things that seemed impossible to others."
- "People tell me I have a large amount of faith."

Marketplace Impact

Prior to becoming the full-time pastor of a church in Houston, Texas, Randy had a successful career as a commercial real estate developer. Faith is one of his primary spiritual gifts.

As a junior project manager early in his career, his company was facing an impossible obstacle. They had the plans and designs to build a golf course on a particular plot of land, but the designs required 3,000,000 cubic yards of dirt. The company did not have the finances to provide enough dirt required. They needed a miracle in the marketplace.

Randy noticed that the city was building a reservoir nearby and that tons of dirt were being excavated in the process. With his God-given gift of faith, he began to speak to those tons of dirt, claiming it for the work his company needed to perform.

Soon, the city officials not only agreed to give the dirt to Randy's company, but they provided all of the means to transport the dirt to the site where the golf course was to be built at no cost to his company. As many as 500 dump trucks dropped loads of dirt in a single day.

By exercising his spiritual gift of faith on behalf of his company, Randy literally saw God move a mountain! As a result, his company's leaders saw the glory of God manifested in the marketplace.

Biblical Insights

- Matthew 8:5-13
- Acts 11:22-24
- Romans 4:18-21
- 1 Corinthians 12:9
- Hebrews 11

Do you have an example of a marketplace Christian who uses the gift of faith in a business setting? To encourage other marketplace Christians who have this gift, please share your example by commenting at the following link where you also will find additional resources and information about how this gift can be used for the glory of God in the marketplace:

www.TheologyofBusiness.com/GiftOfFaith

GIVING

The gift of giving is the special ability to spread the awareness of God's glory by liberally and cheerfully contributing material resources to the work of the Lord.

A marketplace Christian with the spiritual gift of giving might say that marketplace ministry is about "meeting people's needs through creating value in business" and/or "making money to fund the Lord's work."

Gift Recognition Statements

- "I regularly give money beyond my tithe toward the Lord's work."
- "Giving is one of my favorite things to do."
- "People who know me well would say I am a generous person."

Marketplace Impact

Chick-fil-a's founder, Truett Cathy, used his spiritual gift of giving to donate $68 million to over 700 educational and charitable organizations through his company.[1]

Before he died in 2014, Cathy instructed his descendants never to allow the company to go public. Although the company would receive massive financial investment through becoming publically-traded, he knew that the shareholders eventually would reduce the large amount of charitable giving. He also knew that many of the sharcholders would not share his Christian faith, worldview, and values, so the money inevitably would be given to causes misaligned with his value system.

As another expression of his gift of generosity, he also used his company to provide jobs and mentorship for thousands of young people. He founded WinShape specifically to fund college scholarships and Christian discipleship training for many of these young people.

My local Chick-fil-a constantly gives away free food to the community. Recently, they gave away free Chick-fil-a biscuits every Tuesday for an entire month. When I was eating with my family at my local Chick-fil-a restaurant on a recent visit, the manager walked over to give free chocolate chip cookies to us. Truett Cathy's spiritual gift of generosity has been multiplied throughout the culture of Chick-fil-a.

Biblical Insights

- John 12:1-8
- Romans 12:8
- 2 Corinthians 8:1-7; 9:2-7

Do you have an example of a marketplace Christian who uses the gift of giving in a business setting? To encourage other marketplace Christians who have this gift, please share your example by commenting at the following link where you also will find additional resources and information about how this gift can be used for the glory of God in the marketplace:

www.TheologyofBusiness.com/GiftOfGiving

---

[1] http://www.chick-fil-a.com/Company/Responsibility-Overview

HOSPITALITY

The gift of hospitality is the special ability to spread the awareness of God's glory by creating warm and welcoming environments for others.

Gift Recognition Statements

- "I am passionate about helping strangers to feel welcome when they are in my presence."
- "I have invited guests into my home on a regular basis."
- "People often tell me I made them feel welcome in a new place."

Marketplace Impact

John Wanamaker (1838-1922), who is considered the "Father of Modern Advertising," used his spiritual gift of hospitality to revolutionize the shopping experience for people. At the core of his apparent advertising genius was his gift of hospitality. Above all, Wanamaker wanted to welcome as many people as possible into the most comfortable shopping atmosphere possible.

Among his many innovations, Wanamaker opened the world's first major department store because he wanted to provide a store so complete and welcoming that people would not want to leave. In those days, it was unheard of for a store to be a meeting place and even a place for relaxation and enjoyment.

In the fall and winter, Wanamaker had a custom of walking alongside individual customers with a handful of warm chestnuts in his pocket. As they walked together, he would offer the visitor a few of the nuts, and then they would walk, talk, and munch together. His personal hospitality was reflected throughout the entire store and throughout the company's culture.

On the ninth floor of Wanamaker's store was the Crystal Tea Room, a room so extravagantly beautiful and inviting that people have wedding receptions and other major events there to this day. To accommodate the children, the toy department on the eighth floor included a monorail that traveled around the store. For anyone needing medical attention, the tenth floor included in-house physicians and nurses. The store even housed the world's largest playable pipe organ!

At a time when salespeople could charge whatever they could get from their customers because prices were not displayed, Wanamaker introduced price tags to the retail economy, which was the first universal pricing system of its kind. He didn't want people to worry about whether or not they were getting fair prices while they shopped. He wanted his customers to be able to relax and feel welcome in his store.

Ultimately, his gift of hospitality was used to invite people into a relationship with Jesus. When the famous 19th-century evangelist, D.L. Moody, wanted to come to Philadelphia for one of his evangelistic meetings, Wanamaker hosted the event in his store free-of-charge and donated the services of 300 ushers from among his own paid staff to assist with the event.

Deeply committed to personal evangelism, he hand-copied evangelistic letters for each member of his large Sunday school class. The letters read,

If you are not saved, my dear friend, flee to the merciful Savior as you would fly into this warm room tonight, out of the cold streets and the drifting snow. If you are saved, humbly trusting in what Jesus did when his loved failed not on the Cross, think of others not saved... NOT SAVED... going to the eternal darkness—your near friend, your relative—and do something!

Biblical Insights

- Acts 16:14-15
- Romans 12:13; 16:23
- Hebrews 13:1-2
- 1 Peter 4:9

Do you have an example of a marketplace Christian who uses the gift of hospitality in a business setting? To encourage other marketplace Christians who have this gift, please share your example by commenting at the following link where you also will find additional resources and information about how this gift can be used for the glory of God in the marketplace:

www.TheologyofBusiness.com/GiftOfHospitality

Intercessory Prayer

The gift of intercessory prayer is the special ability to spread the awareness of God's glory by praying for extended periods of time on a regular basis in a way that results in frequent and specific answers to those prayers.

Marketplace Christians with the gift of intercessory prayer intercede before God on behalf of their companies and the people with whom they work.

Gift Recognition Statements

- "I am passionate about praying to God on behalf of others."
- "I pray for extended amounts of time concerning the needs in our world."
- "People ask me to pray for them because they know I actually will pray."

Marketplace Impact

Amy Everette is the Chief Prayer Officer of Marketplace ROCK, a consulting company that prays for business executives and their companies while teaching these executives how to intercede on behalf of their companies. One of her clients, a business executive in Boulder, Colorado reported,

> Business intercession has been an integral part of our organization for nearly three years. Our initial purpose of having an intercessor [Amy] on our

team was to help integrate our faith with our business. As a business owner, I am constantly faced with making strategic business decisions for our company. Having a team of intercessors to hear what God is saying about HIS plan for our company is invaluable to us. When you know HIS plan and what season your company is in, strategic decisions become easier to make. We believe that our intercessory team is our unfair advantage, the competitive edge that helps us grow in an industry where many are shrinking. Through recessionary times and corporate challenges, or times of acceleration and growth, our intercessory team is key to the success of our business.[1]

Biblical Insights

- Colossians 1:9-12; 4:12-13
- Hebrews 7:25
- James 5:14-16

Do you have an example of a marketplace Christian who uses the gift of intercessory prayer in a business setting? To encourage other marketplace Christians who have this gift, please share your example by commenting at the following link where you also will find additional resources and information about how this gift can be used for the glory of God in the marketplace:

www.TheologyofBusiness.com/GiftOfIntercessoryPrayer

---

[1] http://www.marketplacerock.com/testimonials/

KNOWLEDGE

The gift of knowledge is the special ability to spread the awareness of God's glory by discovering, accumulating, analyzing, and clarifying information.

Christians with the gift of knowledge have an insatiable hunger to learn.

Gift Recognition Statements

- "My life demonstrates that I am passionate about learning new things."
- "I spend a significant percentage of my time learning new things."
- "People view me as a source of information."

Marketplace Impact

As the founder of market research firm, The Barna Group, George Barna has been using his spiritual gift of knowledge to keep Christians informed about culture-related trends happening in society. Relaying, analyzing, and interpreting responses gathered from opinion polls and other research tools, his company has provided research services for the Disney Channel, ABC, VISA, the U.S. Military, and the Evangelical Christian Community. His research includes findings such as...

- Less than one out of every five born-again adults possesses a Biblical worldview.

- Children are the most important population segment to minister to because of their spiritual teachability and developmental vulnerability.
- The divorce rate among born-again Christians is higher than that for atheists/agnostics.

Biblical Insights

- Acts 5:1-11; 17:11
- 1 Corinthians 12:8
- Colossians 2:2-3

Do you have an example of a marketplace Christian who uses the gift of knowledge in a business setting? To encourage other marketplace Christians who have this gift, please share your example by commenting at the following link where you also will find additional resources and information about how this gift can be used for the glory of God in the marketplace:

www.TheologyofBusiness.com/GiftOfKnowledge

LEADERSHIP

The gift of leadership is the special ability to spread the awareness of God's glory by envisioning that which does not yet exist and then motivating others successfully to work toward the fulfillment of that vision.

When people panic and are looking for direction in the marketplace, they will gravitate toward Christians with the gift of leadership.

Gift Recognition Statements

- "I prefer to focus on the bigger picture while other people work on the details."
- "I am passionate about getting other people involved and leveraging their unique abilities to accomplish large objectives."
- "People often tell me I am a gifted leader."

Marketplace Impact

Ford Taylor is a leader of leaders. Using his spiritual gift of leadership, Ford helped build and then became the CEO of a $300 million sportswear company that had 2000 employees at the time he left to do consulting and leadership training. As the founder of the FSH Group, he now teaches Transformational Leadership to leaders across all spheres of society in multiple U.S. cities and in countries around the world. His clients have ranged from small, private firms to multi-million-dollar corporations.

Ford was blessed with a vision to launch and lead *Transformation Cincinnati and Northern Kentucky*, a city-wide process focused on uniting God's people in businesses, churches, government, education, media, arts, and entertainment through prayer, plans, and actions to spread the Gospel of Jesus. Like others with the gift of leadership, Ford is focused on facilitating transformation. He gets a vision of how things can be, and he leads others toward accomplishing this transformation through the power of God.

Biblical Insights

- Romans 12:8
- 1 Timothy 3:1-13; 5:17
- Hebrews 13:17

Do you have an example of a marketplace Christian who uses the gift of leadership in a business setting? To encourage other marketplace Christians who have this gift, please share your example by commenting at the following link where you also will find additional resources and information about how this gift can be used for the glory of God in the marketplace:

www.TheologyofBusiness.com/GiftOfLeadership

Miracle-Working & Healing

The gifts of healing and miracle-working are the special abilities to spread the awareness of God's glory through altering the natural outcomes of life through God's supernatural power.

The gifts of miracle-working and healing often operate together. Nearly all of the miracles and healings of Jesus recorded in the Gospels occurred in the marketplace, and 39 of the 40 miracles and healings recorded in the Book of Acts occurred in the marketplace.

Gift Recognition Statements

- "I am passionate about pursuing opportunities to see God work miracles wherever I go."
- "I have prayed for specific miracles, signs, wonders, and healings to happen and have seen many of them come to pass."
- "When people need a miracle to happen in their lives, such as a healing miracle, they often ask me to pray for them."

Marketplace Impact

Daniel Gil is a young man who participates in Ninja Warrior, an extremely-difficult and highly-competitive obstacle course contest that is now one of the most popular televised sporting events in the world. He has appeared on national television competing in these contests several times.

Daniel views his platform as a Ninja Warrior contestant as marketplace ministry and an opportunity to use his God-given gifts of miracle-working and healing. God has used him to perform many healing miracles in these Ninja Warrior settings.

In one instance, Daniel was standing in line, waiting for his turn to compete. One of the other contestants in line mentioned that he was experiencing physical pain in his back and did not think he would be able to compete. Feeling compassion for his opponent, Daniel offered to pray for him, which resulted in complete healing. Daniel said,

> I have prayed for dozens of people while at competitions, practices, etc.
>
> Sometimes, I will see a physical ailment and then offer prayer. Other times, people will randomly tell me about injuries that they have been dealing with, and I will offer prayer. Either way, I have prayed for everything from twisted ankles, hurt shoulders, bad backs, knees, elbows, joint pain, headaches, and much much more.
>
> The majority of the healings that I see are ones of miraculously speedy, complete recoveries.
>
> I prayed for a friend from the gym who had been suffering from months of back pain. There was no immediate change after prayer, which discouraged us both a little at the time. But then a few months later, he told me that all the pain had completely left without reason a short time (few weeks) after receiving prayer and has since not come back. He just forgot to tell me!
>
> I prayed for a friend from another city during a local Ninja Warrior competition who had been

suffering from sharp pain in his elbow for 3-4 months. He didn't think he could finish the competition because of the pain, but after prayer, he said there was no more pain and finished the competition! He said it was aggravated that same night while lying in bed but has since not had any- more pain from it and has resumed training on it.

While at a competition, I felt led to pray for a woman's knee. It was in a brace, and she said that she injured it badly while training. After prayer, she said it felt better and that she would be monitoring it to see how quickly it would recover. A few months later, the next time I saw her, she was so excited to tell me that she had just gone running and that recovery went awesome and her knee was feeling great!

I have also gotten to pray for many kids on the Ninja Warrior scene, both in my own gym that I work at and abroad while traveling for competitions and training. I help teach kids' classes throughout the week and as surely as kids get hurt everywhere else in life, they get hurt at the gym occasionally. It's not usually anything serious, but to kids, things always seem worse than they really are. I have gotten to pray for and encourage kids all the time. I'll tell them about how Jesus loves to heal people and that He can take away all the pain they feel. I've had many kids thank me, test it out, feel better, and go back to training, knowing that God is real and just took away their pain.

Biblical Insights

- Acts 3:1-10; 9:32-35; 28:7-10
- 1 Corinthians 12:9-10, 28
- Romans 15:18-19

Do you have an example of a marketplace Christian who uses the gifts of miracle-working and healing in a business setting? To encourage other marketplace Christians who have these gifts, please share your example by commenting at the following link where you also will find additional resources and information about how these gifts can be used for the glory of God in the marketplace:

www.TheologyofBusiness.com/GiftsOfMiraclesAndHealing

Pastoring

The gift of pastoring is the special ability to spread the awareness of God's glory through caring consistently for the personal needs of others through personalized counseling and coaching.

Marketplace Christians with this gift are passionate about meeting the spiritual and emotional needs of their co-workers and other people with whom they interact one-on-one in the marketplace. They listen more than they preach. It is a "ministry of presence," just being available for people.

Gift Recognition Statements

- "I am passionate about connecting with, caring for, and coaching others one-on-one."
- "I often take the time to care for the emotional and/or spiritual needs of people around me."
- "People often share their personal struggles with me because they trust me."

Marketplace Impact

After retiring as a chaplain from the US Army, Gil Stricklin used his spiritual gift of pastoring to begin a chaplain service for companies, which is now known as Marketplace Chaplains USA. Gil saw a need in corporate America for employees to have one-on-one care for their emotional and spiritual needs. Many of these employees would never attend church.

By providing this service, Gil was able to increase employee morale and productivity through displaying the love of Jesus among the employees in his clients' workplaces. Gil's company, Marketplace Chaplains USA, lists the following as benefits of providing pastoral care in the workplace:

- Increases employee retention
- Decreases employee absenteeism
- Increases employee productivity
- Improves workplace safety
- Reduces employee stress
- Increases employee commitment to company goals and objectives
- Reduces employee conflicts
- Increases employee loyalty to the company
- Improves employee attitudes
- Increases employee morale and teamwork
- People feel valued[1]

An employee with one of Marketplace Chaplains USA's clients reported,

> Just the existence of the Chaplain Care Team at David Weekley Homes (Six-Time Honoree on *Fortune Magazine's* list of "The Best Companies to Work For") helps to set the tone for the level of integrity and morals expected from its people. It was one of the items that really attracted me to David Weekley Homes because it showed me that he had a vested interest in my overall well-being, not just in what I could do for the company.[2]

Biblical Insights

- John 10:1-18
- Ephesians 4:11-14
- 1 Timothy 3:1-7
- 1 Peter 5:1-3

Do you have an example of a marketplace Christian who uses the gift of pastoring in a business setting? To encourage other marketplace Christians who have this gift, please share your example by commenting at the following link where you also will find additional resources and information about how this gift can be used for the glory of God in the marketplace:

www.TheologyofBusiness.com/GiftOfPastoring

---

[1] http://mchapusa.com/benefits/

[2] Ibid.

PROPHECY

The gift of prophecy is the special ability to spread the awareness of God's glory through confronting people with the truth concerning their faulty thinking and behavior.

Gift Recognition Statements

- "I don't mind confronting people about their faulty thinking."
- "I have communicated to others timely and urgent messages that I believe came directly from God."
- "Other people have confirmed that they believe I speak God's truth about specific situations."

Marketplace Impact

David Giuseppetti has used his spiritual gift of prophecy as an equipment technician in the oil industry for several decades. On at least one occasion, using his gift of prophecy saved a man's life.

Back in 2013, David was maintaining equipment on an oil rig during a 28-day assignment in a remote part of Papua New Guinea. One day at work, he noticed that crew members were walking nearby and even under the automated pipe-handling equipment that was hoisting 10,000-pound pipes. David said, "God put a recurring uneasiness in my heart. And I understood that if I didn't do anything about this, an accident was going to occur."

David immediately alerted the drilling company's safety coordinator about the hazardous situation, but no precautions were taken after the safety coordinator mentioned David's concern at a leaders' meeting.

Sensing that God had given to him a mandate to proclaim this warning until the necessary actions were taken, David then elevated the issue to the company's top safety manager. The safety manager responded, "I'll see what I can do." In the end, nothing was done.

After 15 days of persistently warning the company's leaders about the problem, David shared the warning with the rig manager, the highest authority on the oil rig. The rig manager agreed that the hazard presented a threat to the safety of the crew members. He immediately authorized David to block off the area with a chain and a few warning signs. After David took the necessary steps to designate the hazardous area, he left the rig and went to the company's camp about five miles away.

When David returned the following day, the rig manager pointed at David and proclaimed, "Here he comes! Give him a round of applause!" All 300 crewmembers began to applaud. Next to the rig manager was standing David's co-worker and close friend, a former rugby player for the New Zealand All Blacks. David's friend explained that, on the night before, he was going to weld a piece of metal as he often did. He went to cross under the machine, but when he saw the chain and the warning signs, he immediately turned to take an alternate route. At that exact moment when he turned, one of the 10,000-pound pipes fell from the automated pipe-handler from 80 feet above and landed only two feet away from where David's friend was walking. He told David that his life was saved because David had installed the chain and the warning signs.

As a result of speaking forth and acting on the prophetic message God had given to him, the life of David's friend—a husband and father to two children—was saved.

Biblical Insights

- Acts 11:27-28
- 1 Corinthians 12:10; 14:1-4
- 1 Thessalonians 1:5

Do you have an example of a marketplace Christian who uses the gift of prophecy in a business setting? To encourage other marketplace Christians who have this gift, please share your example by commenting at the following link where you also will find additional resources and information about how this gift can be used for the glory of God in the marketplace:

www.TheologyofBusiness.com/GiftOfProphecy

SERVICE

The gift of service is the special ability to spread the awareness of God's glory by performing supportive tasks with great joy, eagerness, and effectiveness.

Gift Recognition Statements

- "I am eager to help even when others are not."
- "I enjoy doing the tasks my leaders don't have time to do."
- "People around me know they can count on me to help out."

Marketplace Impact

In his classic book, *Business by the Book*, Larry Burkett told the story of Will, the owner of a large manufacturing company who displayed a supernatural level of service toward a staff member who betrayed him. Although Will had invested five years of time and resources grooming his plant manager to become the next president of the company, the plant manager submitted his resignation one day without any explanation.

When Will asked the plant manager, John, to stay only long enough for the company to find a replacement, John refused.

Nevertheless, Will forgave John and prayed for him regularly. Will hosted a going away party for John and provided a substantial severance bonus.

Three months later, John opened his own company and copied Will's best-selling product. Soon, John's company had become one of Will's largest competitors.

Nine years later, Will learned that there had been a design problem with one of John's new products and that he was facing several lawsuits as a result.

With a forgiving, servant's heart, Will bought one of John's products, tested it, pinpointed the problem, and commissioned his engineers to find the solution. Once the solution had been determined, Will called John to explain how he could fix the problem to satisfy his customers.[1] Indeed, he went the "extra mile" in his service to John.

Biblical Insights

- Mark 15:40-41
- Acts 6:1-7; 9:36
- Romans 12:7; 16:1-2
- 1 Corinthians 12:28
- Galatians 6:10
- 1 Timothy 1:16-18
- Titus 3:14

Do you have an example of a marketplace Christian who uses the gift of service in a business setting? To encourage other marketplace Christians who have this gift, please share your example by commenting at the following link where you also will find additional resources and information about how this gift can be used for the glory of God in the marketplace:

www.TheologyofBusiness.com/GiftOfService

---

[1] Larry Burkett, *Business by the Book* (Nashville: Thomas Nelson, 1998), 4.

TEACHING

The gift of teaching is the special ability to spread the awareness of God's glory by communicating information in a way that the hearers can understand and apply it.

Gift Recognition Statements

- "I am passionate about putting in the extra effort to explain complicated concepts in a simple way so that people can understand."
- "I teach everywhere I go... not just in a classroom setting."
- "People have told me I am a good teacher."

Marketplace Impact

Leslie Samuel uses his spiritual gift of teaching as the biology instructor for his educational website, Interactive-Biology.com. At the time of this writing, his easy-to-understand biology tutorials are being used by as many as 75,000 people in a month.

Leslie uses his teaching gift as a platform for giving glory to God. He said, "What I've accomplished is because of one simple reason – God has been good to me!"[1] His fun and down-to-earth teaching style invites people to learn about biology from him, opening the door for him to share and teach about his love for God.

Having learned from the success of his Interactive Biology website, he also uses his teaching gift through another educational website, BecomeABlogger.com, which helps people start and grow a blog that can make a positive impact on the world. As he shared in his blogpost, "Where in the World Are the Christian Internet Marketers?", he is on a quest to encourage other Christian internet marketing teachers to use their platforms for the glory of God.[2]

Biblical Insights

- Acts 18:24-28; 20:20-21
- 1 Corinthians 12:28
- Ephesians 4:11-14

Do you have an example of a marketplace Christian who uses the gift of teaching in a business setting? To encourage other marketplace Christians who have this gift, please share your example by commenting at the following link where you also will find additional resources and information about how this gift can be used for the glory of God in the marketplace:

www.TheologyofBusiness.com/GiftOfTeaching

---

[1] http://www.becomeablogger.com/aboutme/

[2] http://www.becomeablogger.com/4243/christian-internet-marketers/

Tongues & Interpretation

The gifts of tongues and interpretation are the special abilities to spread the awareness of God's glory by speaking to God, to one's self, or to others in an unknown, heavenly language in a way that people are edified spiritually.

Gift Recognition Statements

- "I often speak to God in a language I have never learned."
- "To strengthen myself spiritually, I speak to my spirit regularly in an unknown, heavenly language."
- "I have spoken a message from God to others in an unknown, heavenly language that I or someone else interpreted."

Marketplace Impact

Brian "Head" Welch was ranked No. 26 on *Guitar World's* list of the "100 Greatest Heavy Metal Guitarists of All Time."[1] His band, Korn, had sold more than 35 million records as of 2012.[2]

In 2005, Brian became a born-again Christian and subsequently left the band to focus on his relationship with Jesus, being a father, getting free from his severe drug addiction, and launching his solo music career. He rejoined Korn as a Christ-follower in 2013. Brian's transition from using his influence and musical talents for selfish ambition and self-indulgence into using his influence and talents for the glory of God required far more than will power and good intentions.

In his memoir, *Save Me from Myself,* Brian explained that his spiritual gift and practice of speaking in tongues "was a big part of [his] deliverance." He went on to say that the gift of tongues is "part of [his] life everyday now." Despite being advised by his mother and brother to avoid talking about the gift of tongues in his book, he felt compelled to include it because it is a part of who God made him to be. It is one of his spiritual gifts God entrusted to him to overcome his drug addiction, accomplish things that will last in eternity, and spread the awareness of Jesus throughout the music industry and beyond. He explained,

> Here is my opinion on speaking in tongues: If you want to have the most faith you can have on this earth, learn to pray in tongues. If you find it too weird and you prefer to live a good, quiet Christian life, don't pray in tongues. It's just that simple. It all comes down to personal choice, just like everything else in life. God will love you the same whether you pray in tongues or not.

In 2008, Brian became a representative of The Whosoevers, a group of influential musicians, artists, and athletes dedicated to sharing "hope, life, and love" through a worldwide movement centered on Jesus.

Biblical Insights

- 1 Corinthians 12:10; 14:1-14

Do you have an example of a marketplace Christian who uses the gifts of tongues and interpretation in a business setting? To encourage other marketplace Christians who have these gifts, please share your example by commenting at the following link where you also will find additional resources and information about how these gifts can be used for the glory of God in the marketplace:

www.TheologyofBusiness.com/GiftsOfTonguesAndInterpretation

---

[1] Eric Olsen, "Guitar World's '100 Greatest Metal Guitarists of All Time'" (February 1, 2004), http://blogcritics.org/guitar-worlds-100-greatest-metal-guitarists/.

[2] Sonakshi Babbar, "Metal Mayhem: Korn to Raise Hell in Delhi," *HindustanTimes.com*, (September 4, 2012), http://www.hindustantimes.com/music/metal-mayhem-korn-to-raise-hell-in-delhi/article1-924367.aspx.

Wisdom

The gift of wisdom is the special ability to spread the awareness of God's glory by bringing clarity to specific situations through the application of God's truth.

The gift of wisdom is different than the gift of knowledge. Not only do Christians with the gift of wisdom know the truth, they know how to *apply* it to specific situations in everyday life.

Marketplace Christians with the spiritual gift of wisdom are gifted to apply the wisdom of God to specific business situations. God has given to us the Holy Spirit to lead us "into all truth," and He has given to us His Word, which is full of timeless business wisdom.

Gift Recognition Statements

- "I intuitively find solutions to complicated problems."
- "I apply the truth of God's Word in my everyday life."
- "People often ask me how to deal with confusing situations."

Marketplace Impact

Dave Ramsey uses his spiritual gift of wisdom to help people solve financial problems in accordance with the wisdom of God. Although he refers to the advice he shares on his radio talk show as "common sense for your dollars and cents," the wisdom he shares with his callers does not seem to be very common.

As people came to hear the wisdom of Solomon thousands of years ago, people call in to the *Dave Ramsey Show* to ask Dave for wisdom concerning specific financial issues they are facing. Through his radio shows, books, and live events, the advice he shares is inspired and informed by biblical principles concerning money and business.

When I was 26, I was $26,000 in debt: student loans, an auto loan, credit card debt, and even a loan to buy an expensive guitar. During that time, I read Dave Ramsey's book, *Total Money Makeover*. Though I had made almost no progress toward paying off my debt prior to reading Dave's book, I paid-off my $26,000 debt entirely within 12 months after reading it. Dave Ramsey's spiritual gift of wisdom helped me to change my life through the power of the Holy Spirit.

Biblical Insights

- Acts 6:3, 10
- 1 Corinthians 2:6-13; 12:8

Do you have an example of a marketplace Christian who uses the gift of wisdom in a business setting? To encourage other marketplace Christians who have this gift, please share your example by commenting at the following link where you also will find additional resources and information about how this gift can be used for the glory of God in the marketplace:

www.TheologyofBusiness.com/GiftOfWisdom

Worship

The gift of worship is the special ability to spread the awareness of God's glory by being keenly aware of the presence, majesty, and goodness of God and to invoke God's presence into one's daily life.

Marketplace Christians with the gift of worship invite the presence of God into their workplaces. They recognize that the Bible teaches us to do our work "as unto the Lord" (Col. 3:23) as our work is a primary means by which we worship God. They also help others around them to become aware of God's presence, majesty, and goodness.

Gift Recognition Statements

- "Throughout the day, I am keenly aware of the presence, majesty, and goodness of God."
- "I set apart time every day to worship God and invite His presence into my life and into the atmosphere around me wherever I go."
- "Others have told me I helped to lead them into the presence of God."

Marketplace Impact

Shae Bynes uses her spiritual gift of worship in her marketplace role as a coach and teacher on Christ-centered business and marriage. She is the author of 10 books.

Shae wrote her first two books before she learned to activate her gift of worship in the writing process. For Shae, writing those first two books "felt like a grind" because she had not yet learned to worship God through her work.

Over the course of writing her next eight books, she refused to write without the accompaniment of her "Holy Ghostwriter." She reported,

> I speak to Him before I start writing. I thank Him for who He is. I thank Him for the opportunity to minister to others through writing. I tell Him that I'm yielded and ready for what He wants to share through me. I also play my favorite worship music in the background while I'm writing because it helps keep my heart and mind focused on Him. Of course, that means I sometimes end up crying in the middle of writing or have to take a break to just worship (because I can't lift my hands and type at the same time). But then, I get back to the flow of writing.
>
> I have found that my sweet spot for writing is between 1am-5am, and I usually write in 3-4 hour sessions. During that time, I'll honor Him, and whenever He nudges me to go a certain direction or to dig deeper on a topic, I thank Him for leading me and ask Him where He wants me to go to dig deeper. It's basically an ongoing conversation. I do tend to talk out loud, but sometimes, I'll just ask Him without speaking aloud.

She continued, "I ask Him to give me His heart concerning those who will be reading the book, and He always delivers."

Shae's gift of worship carries over into her live business training events. After a recent training event, one of the attendees reported,

> There is no earthy language sophisticated enough to describe what transpired at the event. It was indeed a 21st century "Day of Pentecost" new birth experience for marketplace leaders.[1]

Shae explained, "His manifested presence met us there that weekend. People were healed, delivered, restored, reaffirmed, and repositioned."

Biblical Insights

- Deuteronomy 31:22
- 1 Samuel 16:16, 23
- 1 Chronicles 16:41-42
- 2 Chronicles 5:12-13; 34:12
- Psalm 150
- Luke 10:38-42

Do you have an example of a marketplace Christian who uses the gift of worship in a business setting? To encourage other marketplace Christians who have this gift, please share your example by commenting at the following link where you also will find additional resources and information about how this gift can be used for the glory of God in the marketplace:

www.TheologyofBusiness.com/GiftOfWorship

[1] Shae Bynes and Antonina Geer, *The Firestarter Effect: Making Jesus Christ Known in the Marketplace* (Lauderhill, FL: Kingdom Driven, 2014).

MULTIPLYING THE IMPACT OF YOUR SPIRITUAL GIFTS

AS MOSES STOOD BEFORE GOD at the burning bush, God asked him, "What's that in your hand?" (Exod. 4:2)

Moses replied, "It's my staff."

God then commanded him to throw it on the ground before the burning bush.

Although it may have seemed like just a simple stick to us, Moses' staff represented his identity as a shepherd. It also represented his livelihood because his wealth was linked directly to livestock. Finally, the staff represented his gift of leadership as he used the staff to guide his sheep.

Having cast his rod on the ground before the presence of God, Moses symbolically was surrendering his identity, his livelihood, and his God-given gifts back to God as one complete and living sacrifice.

Full surrender to God is the prerequisite for understanding our spiritual gifts, understanding how God wants to use them, and using them to their fullest potential. We are called to surrender our bodies as "living sacrifices, holy and pleasing to God, so that [we] may prove what the will of God is, that which is good and acceptable and perfect" (Rom. 12:1-2). The realization of what has been made available to us by the Spirit of God—that is, proving "what the will of God is"—only occurs when we submit our lives to Him completely. A sacrifice is only ignited by the Spirit of God when it is first laid upon His altar.

When Moses took up his rod again after casting it before the burning bush, the staff turned into a snake. God was showing Moses that there was something deceptive inside of him that had the potential to rob him of his full reliance on God, thus sabotaging his participation in God's plan for his life.

As we surrender our lives to God on a daily basis in the marketplace, He will reveal the "snakes" inside us that could prevent us from participating in His purposes and from tapping into His power. These "snakes" cause us to rely on our own strength and abilities to succeed within the systems of the world. They prevent us from participating in the Holy Spirit's mission to spread the awareness of Jesus, God's glory, throughout the earth. We must surrender our lives to God on a daily basis in order to become supernaturally empowered with the help of God.

From the time when Moses took up his staff the second time, Moses—writing the *Book of Exodus* under the inspiration of the Holy Spirit—began to refer to it as "the staff of God" because he had made the decision to surrender his identity, livelihood, and gifts to the will and power of God (Exod. 4:20). This was the same rod that Moses extended over the Red Sea, parting the waters to save his people from the Egyptian army.

As God questioned Moses, He also is asking you, "What's in *your* hand?" God will use all of your strengths, weaknesses, experiences, and circumstances to fulfill His purpose for your life. He will use your past, present, and future. The Bible says, "We know that God causes all things to work together for good to those who love God and are called according to His purpose" (Rom.

8:28). He will derive glory from even the most unlikely aspects of our lives.

The impact of whatever you surrender to His purposes will be multiplied exponentially. Just as Jesus fed 5,000 families with merely five loaves of bread and two fish and as surely as Moses parted the Red Sea by holding up a simple stick that became "the staff of God," God will use "all things" in your past, present, and future to perform wonders for His glory, your benefit, and for the benefits of others. Allow God to use the spiritual gifts He has given to you to spread the awareness of Jesus throughout your sphere of influence in the marketplace and beyond.

Group Discussion: Have you fully surrendered your spiritual gifts back to the Holy Spirit so He can use them for the glory of God?

ABOUT THE AUTHOR

Darren Shearer is the podcast host and lead blogger for *Theology of Business*, a training organization that helps marketplace Christians to partner with God in business to make disciples of their co-workers, companies, and industries. He is the author of three books, including *Marketing Like Jesus: 25 Strategies to Change the World.*

Darren is the founder and CEO of High Bridge Books (www.HighBridgeBooks.com), which offers professional book publishing services for inspiring thought leaders.

A former Captain in the United States Air Force, Darren earned the United States Air Force Commendation Medal for his meritorious service in Kuwait during Operation Iraqi Freedom.

He holds a M.A. in Practical Theology from Regent University (Virginia Beach, VA), an Advanced Graduate Certificate in Management from Pace University (New York, NY), and a B.A. in English from Charleston Southern University (Charleston, SC).

He and his wife, Marie, reside in Houston, Texas and have two young boys: Solomon and Armand.

To connect with Darren or to contact him about speaking at an upcoming event, you may contact him via the following:

E-mail: Darren@HighBridgeBooks.com

Web: www.TheologyofBusiness.com/contact

Twitter: @DarrenShearer

Facebook: www.Facebook.com/BusinessTheology

AVAILABLE IN PAPERBACK AND E-BOOK
AT THEOLOGYOFBUSINESS.COM
AND AMAZON.COM

THEOLOGY
of
BUSINESS

with
Darren Shearer